CONTEMPORARY NEW MEXICO,
1940–1990

CONTEMPORARY NEW MEXICO, 1940–1990

EDITED BY
RICHARD W. ETULAIN

UNIVERSITY OF NEW MEXICO PRESS
ALBUQUERQUE

IN COOPERATION WITH THE
UNIVERSITY OF NEW MEXICO
CENTER FOR THE AMERICAN WEST

Library of Congress Cataloging in Publication Data
Contemporary New Mexico, 1940–1990 / edited by Richard W. Etulain. —
1st ed.
    p.   cm.
    "In cooperation with the University of New Mexico, Center for the
American West."
    Includes bibliographical references and index.
    ISBN 0-8263-1486-4 (pbk.)
    1. New Mexico—Civilization—20th century. I. Etulain, Richard
W. 11. University of New Mexico. Center for the American West.
F801.2.C66 1994
978.9'05—dc20   93-32426
                                                CIP

Designed by Linda Mae Tratechaud

CONTENTS

ILLUSTRATIONS

PREFACE

IN the last generation or so, westerners have discovered their twentieth-century history. Previously tied to a frontier or Wild West interpretation of their past, they failed to examine the complex and swiftly changing region that emerged after 1900. But, beginning in the 1960s and 1970s, historians like Earl Pomeroy and Gerald D. Nash and journalists such as Neil Morgan and Neal R. Peirce, in several provocative and thorough volumes, demonstrated the importance of comprehending the modern West. All of these writers noted the signal importance of the Second World War in western history. In fact, one or two suggested that the world-shaking events of the early 1940s have done more than any other occurrence to shape the identity of the modern American West.

More recently, other authors have pushed ahead to discuss the large influences of World War II and the 1960s on the contemporary West. In nearly all of these accounts, writers emphasize the central importance of race and ethnicity, families, and the environment in understanding recent developments within the region. For the first time, major dimensions of the post-1940 West are now coming into clear focus.

These cultural and intellectual trends obviously influence the content and form of the essays included in this pioneering volume. Although encouraged to center on a specific topic, authors have viewed their topics in larger contexts, sometimes revealing national and even international influences on New Mexico and the Southwest. Nor will readers fail to notice the important roles that ethnicity, gender, and the environment play throughout this volume. Still, while emphasizing these now-familiar topics, contributors also point out the unique social and cultural mixes resulting in New Mexico when, for example, peoples of persisting cultures and long traditions come in contact with federal power, the latest scientific developments, and new border influences.

Overall, the goal of this volume is twofold: to supply a brief overview of New Mexico during the last half-century and to suggest how dozens of important subjects of this fifty-year period remain to be studied. In the opening essay, distinguished historian Gerald D. Nash, drawing upon his extensive research on the modern West, furnishes a brief overview of New Mexico since 1940. In the next chapter, F. Chris Garcia, leading expert on recent politics, demonstrates the continuing complexities of New Mexico politics and government. Michael Welsh then adds important information on economic trends in the state during the last five decades.

In the second half of the volume, three scholars provide helpful overviews of families, ethnic experiences, and cultural trends in New Mexico. Social historian Virginia Scharff appealingly personalizes the changes and dilemmas facing families in the state, whereas Rosalie Otero examines ethnic diversity in recent New Mexico, particularly as revealed through its literature and art. In the final essay, Ferenc Szasz surveys both elite and popular cultural developments, suggesting the richness of that field for future investigations. To each section is appended a bibliography of suggested further readings pertinent to that topic.

These essays were first presented at a well-attended conference on the campus of the University of New Mexico in February 1992. Cosponsored by the History Department and College of Arts and Sciences and funded in part by the New Mexico Endowment for the Humanities, that gathering encouraged the editor and contributors to make their essays available in published form. For support and financial assistance along the way, the Center for the American West is indebted to B. Hobson Wildenthal, then dean of the College of Arts and Sciences; Jonathan Porter, chair of the Department of History, and John Lucas, executive director of the NMEH. We are also grateful to Dick Knipfing and Darlis Miller for their parts in the conference. The editor wishes to express his special thanks to staff members at the Center for their help in planning the conference and in preparing this volume. Pat Devejian not only organized much of the conference, she typed portions of the manuscript and read proof. Jon Hunner helped with planning and selection of photographs. Traci Hukill aided in choosing photographs, read proof, and helped compile the index. Jill Howard likewise read proof. My daughter Jackie also proofread several essays and worked on the index. I am very grateful for all their help.

Richard W. Etulain
Spring 1993

ONE

NEW MEXICO SINCE 1940

AN OVERVIEW

GERALD D. NASH

IN 1990 the U.S. Census reminded us that New Mexico had grown to encompass a population of about 1.5 million inhabitants, a majority of them living in urban areas. That simple statement of fact calls attention to the many changes that the state has undergone in the course of the last century. But to comprehend the significance of this period, however, it needs to be considered within the broader context of New Mexico's history, and not merely in terms of years, but of centuries.

BEFORE 1940

From the perspective of the 1990s, New Mexico evolved through at least five stages. The first of these embraced the span of the Anasazi culture, when the predecessors of present-day Pueblo peoples settled in the Southwest, perhaps as early as 1500 B.C. Most were nomadic hunters in the region for about one thousand years. About 500 B.C., they were succeeded by people who developed more stable forms of agriculture, such as corn and squash, and built fairly extensive irrigation works. They also constructed extensive stone and cliff dwellings by the first years of the Christian era. Archaeologists report that they developed sophisticated social and economic institutions, reflected in the first true pottery as well as in bows and arrows from this period. In addition, these people were skilled basket makers, who were also adept in the fabrication of musical instruments and of a wide range of tools. By about 700 A.D. their communal houses had grown so much that they resembled small towns. These communities flourished for another six hundred years or so. Sometime about 1300, drought conditions led many of the inhabitants to abandon the area. With their departure, our knowledge of their consequent fate becomes obscure. They vanished from the screen of history.

The coming of the Spaniards in the sixteenth century inaugurated another phase of New Mexico's history. When Francisco de Coronado first visited the area in 1540 and claimed it for the Spanish crown, he found Pueblo villages that were more than two hundred years old. For the next 281 years New Mexico was under Spanish rule. During this period Spanish missionary activities left an imprint, although the well-established pueblo communities continued to function. Both bequeathed an economic, social, and religious legacy to later generations. The Franciscan fathers brought Christianity; the Spanish crown made substantial land grants that created a pastoral economy emphasizing stock raising and some farming; and small farmers, including Native Americans, engaged in agriculture and some mining. Although a few small villages grew, such as Santa Fe, Albuquerque, and Las Cruces, this was primarily a pastoral society. But the Spaniards were not primarily a colonizing people, and found New Mexico disappointing because it did not yield large hoards of precious metals, unlike Mexico and Peru. Thus, the population of New Mexico in the seventeenth and eighteenth centuries rarely exceeded twenty-five thousand people. When the Spanish Franciscan, Fray Marcos de Niza first saw the seven pueblos of the Zuni Indians in 1539,

Taos pueblo is one of the oldest inhabited pueblos in the Southwest. (Courtesy Center for Southwest Research, General Library, University of New Mexico, neg. no. 000-478-3299.)

he reported that he had found the Seven Cities of Cibola, which were rumored to hold great wealth and unlimited treasure. But succeeding years proved that his vision was erroneous. New Mexico remained poor and isolated, troubled by sporadic revolts (such as the Pueblo Revolt of 1680) of the Pueblo Indians against repressive Spanish rule. New Mexico grew but little in the two centuries after its first discovery by Europeans.

In 1821, New Mexico entered a third phase of its history when Mexico won its independence from Spain and made New Mexico one of its provinces. Yet the transfer of ownership did not greatly affect everyday life in the remote area. Communication with Mexico City was too irregular to allow Mexican officials to exercise much authority in their northern domains. Life in New Mexico went on much as before. But east and north of New Mexico great changes were in the offing during these years, as a young United States embarked on an intensive period of expansion—driven by a belief in its Manifest Destiny to rule much of the continent.

Initially, the Mexican government was amenable to closer contacts with its North American neighbor. In 1821, it opened trade with the United States via the Santa Fe Trail—a route that wended its way from Missouri to New Mexico—pointing the way also to California. Each year the contacts between New Mexicans and Americans between 1822 and 1846 increased. Americans brought manufactured goods that previously had been unavailable in New Mexico and that were greatly desired by its isolated inhabitants. Americans, on the other hand, found new opportunities for trade and commerce. Thus, New Mexico's population grew slowly during these years as Americans now settled there, founding new enterprises, such as grist mills, and providing new employment opportunities, as in the general stores they opened. But, as elsewhere, when American settlers moved into sparsely inhabited areas they wanted their government to follow. Their restless urges increased their land hunger, which contributed to the war with Mexico in 1846. Under the Treaty of Guadalupe Hidalgo of 1848, the United States acquired much of the Southwest and California, including New Mexico.

As part of the United States, New Mexico now entered a fourth phase of its development. Initially, American ownership did not result in dramatic changes. New Mexico was still isolated and remote, far removed from the rest of the United States. Its population and its economy grew only slowly between 1850 and 1880. By the latter year it had perhaps 119,000 people, of whom one-half were Hispanic. But its expansion accelerated in 1880, when one of the great new transcontinental railroad lines—the Atchison, Topeka and Santa Fe Railroad—finally reached into the territory, binding it to the rest of the nation. The coming of the railroad accelerated population growth and economic development. By 1912 New Mexico finally had more than the 60,000 inhabitants (327,000 according to the Census of 1910) necessary to qualify it for statehood. From then until 1940 the state grew rather slowly, increasing its population to 532,000 by the eve of World War II.

World War II did much to transform this charming multicultural society. In the next half-century the population grew threefold. The economy became increasingly diversified. From a relatively homogeneous society of Hispanics, Native Americans, and Anglos, which had characterized New Mexico since 1850, the state came to include different ethnic and racial groups, including African-Americans and Americans of a wide range of ethnic backgrounds. Instead of a characteristic rural population and life-style, war experiences ushered in urbanization in northern, central, and southern regions of the state. At the same time, the state experienced a real cultural boom. Building on the influx of artists and writers in the 1920s and 1930s, it became home to large numbers of artists and art galleries, and to an active musical life featuring opera, symphonies, and choral and chamber music. Attendance at its schools and universities also increased more than tenfold. In 1940 New Mexico was far removed from most scientific activities in the United States. Fifty years later its scientific installations enjoyed worldwide renown, and it boasted a sizable group of scientific researchers. In a myriad of ways, the war had significantly transformed New Mexico and the life-styles of its inhabitants.

Viewed against the background of thirty-four hundred years of New Mexico history, the period from 1940 to 1990 was clearly the most dynamic era in the state's long history. No other period witnessed such dramatic changes and such dramatic growth—for good or ill. Perhaps only the coming of the Spaniards in the sixteenth century can rival World War II as providing a major turning point in New Mexico's history.

1940–1990

What were the major influences that profoundly influenced New Mexico from 1940 to 1990? Let us consider six keys to an understanding of New Mexico's growth between 1940 and 1990.

First, wars did much to shape the state's development—both in World War II and, then, during the Cold War. Second, government expenditures for a wide array of programs have played a large, even a decisive, role. Third, science and technology modified life in New Mexico, as they did in much of the rest of the nation. Fourth, the geographical-environmental characteristics of the state have continued to exert an influence on its development—even when modified by technology. Fifth, New Mexico's unique amalgam of peoples—old settlers and new—gave its society a distinctive character. That character was marked by conflicts as well as by accommodation. Sixth, the affluence that characterized American life during much of this period undoubtedly also affected New Mexico's growth. Certainly, these six influences are not the only ones that could be considered, but they contribute to a fuller understanding of the state's development.

First, let us consider the influence of World War II, which had an enormous impact on New Mexico as it had on other areas in the West. To be sure, New Mexico did not experience a population boom, as California and the Pacific Coast did. But the war did change population trends in the state, and Hispanics were significantly affected. Their patriotism was reflected in their high rate of enlistment in the armed forces, a rate notably above the national average. The most popular branch for Hispanics entering military service was the paratrooper corps. New job opportunities on the Pacific Coast also attracted many young men and women from the small villages of northern New Mexico, where employment opportunities were limited. The census estimated that fully one-third of young Hispanic men under twenty-five years of age left northern New Mexico during the war to seek work outside the state. One effect of the war, therefore, was to hasten the decline of the small, self-sufficient farm in New Mexico.

The war had an even greater influence on many Native Americans in New Mexico. They too joined the military services in significant numbers. Perhaps as many as one-third left the reservations to seek jobs in war industries on the West Coast, and California shipyards were a popular destination. Those who remained in New Mexico found new economic opportunities at home. Thus, about fifteen hundred Navajos worked in constructing expanded facilities at Fort Wingate (near Gallup), as the army converted it into a large supply depot to serve the Pacific war. Others met the desperate need for field labor and helped in the harvesting of crops. Some were engaged in track maintenance for the Santa Fe Railroad. And the Pueblo tribes living near Los Alamos—as at Santo Domingo—found various employment opportunities there that had not been available before 1940. The net result of these intercultural contacts was profound. Wartime conditions disrupted the Native American barter economy and brought the tribes into a cash economy. It also widened the gap between traditionalists and modernists on the reservations, as military service and wartime jobs expanded the world in which Indians lived. At the end of the war at least one-third of those who had left the reservations chose not to return, but went to live in New Mexico towns and cities.

The war also heightened the political and racial consciousness of New Mexico's Native Americans. No longer were they prone to accept second-class citizenship. Wartime experiences bred a new class of Native American leaders who strove actively to involve their people in the state's political process. This included the attainment of voting rights (not granted by the New

Mexico legislature until 1948) and office holding. The first Indians
in the New Mexico legislature did not appear until 1962.

And the war wrought a veritable revolution in Native
American attitudes toward education. Before 1940 most Indians were suspicious of white-dominated schools because they
perceived—quite accurately—that such training could dilute
the language abilities and cultural inheritance of their children.
But wartime experiences persuaded a large number of Native
Americans that education, at all levels, was a key to mobility
in American society and to improving conditions under which
most of them lived. After 1945, therefore, Native American
tribes in New Mexico encouraged their youth to secure a public
school education, to attend colleges and universities, and also
to enter professions like law, medicine, nursing, business, and
engineering. World War II thus had an important impact on the
Native Americans of New Mexico.

The war had a notable effect in making New Mexico a
center of advanced scientific research in the nation. Before 1940
New Mexico did not have extensive scientific institutions. A
notable exception was the experiments of Dr. Robert H. Goddard,
one of the world's preeminent rocketry pioneers. Seeking an
area that offered mild climates and wide-open spaces suitable
for rocket testing, Goddard settled on a Mescalero ranch near
Roswell in 1930. During the next decade he conducted successful tests with liquid-fueled rockets, until 1941 when he went
east. But the war stimulated establishment of the Manhattan
Project and the construction of a major science laboratory at Los
Alamos. That brought together the world's greatest scientists,
men like its director, Robert Oppenheimer, Enrico Fermi, and
Edward Teller. Most left in 1945, after their development of the
world's first atomic bomb, but they succeeded in giving Los
Alamos Laboratories a worldwide reputation. The war thus had
unforeseen effects in creating a network of scientists and

On July 16, 1945, the first atomic bomb was detonated in the desert near Alamogordo. (Courtesy National Atomic Museum, Albuquerque, NM.)

scientific laboratories in New Mexico, where there had been very few before.

The war also stimulated the establishment of military installations in New Mexico, which contributed increasingly to the state's economy. These included Kirtland Air Force Base, created in 1941. It was soon joined by the establishment of a large weapons-development facility. In the eastern part of the state, the air force established Cannon Air Force Base, near which Clovis quickly became a major contributor to the economy of that part of the state. That was also true of Walker Air Force Base, an important testing facility near Roswell. Explosion of the atomic bomb near Alamogordo in southern New Mexico on July 16, 1945, called attention to the potentials of that area as a testing facility for rockets and advanced missiles. That resulted in the creation of the Holloman Air Force Base and the White Sands Missile Range (originally a proving ground) and weapons-research laboratory near Alamogordo.

World War II thus generated changes for New Mexico in various ways. It disrupted the rural life-styles of many of its peoples. It hastened assimilation and also greater racial consciousness among Hispanics and Native Americans. And it brought New Mexico a new scientific complex and extensive new military installations.

Although the Second World War ended in 1945, it was quickly followed by the Cold War (1945–89), as Americans entered upon an uneasy peace with the Soviet Union. To be sure, New Mexico was far removed from areas of conflict around the world, but its development was directly affected by the Cold War, punctuated by two large-scale, costly hot wars— in Korea (1950–53) and in Viet Nam (1965–73).

How did the Cold War affect New Mexico? In the first place, it resulted in the maintenance and expansion of military and testing installations. Second, it led Congress to authorize increasingly larger federal expenditures for science and technological research. Third, these policies resulted in significant demographic changes, as they brought an influx of new people to New Mexico, including a large number of scientists from all parts of the United States. That, in turn, triggered a boom in housing and construction and underlay a striking growth in urban development.

Essentially, the general influence of the Cold War on New Mexico was to generate a vast amount of new investment capital to fuel the state's growth. A significant portion of such funds came from the federal government. For over a century the lack of such investment monies had hampered New Mexico's expansion. The Cold War afforded New Mexico the opportunity whereby the federal government felt justified to make extensive commitments. Precise estimates of the total of such investments await detailed studies in the future. An uneducated guess would fix on a total sum of between 75 and 100 billion dollars during the years between 1945 and 1990. It is doubtful that Congress would have authorized the spending of such large sums in the state if it had not been for the heated passions and fears stirred by the Cold War.

In contrast to the First World War, Congress did not close or abandon military installations after World War II. It closed temporary bases at Hobbs, Deming, and Fort Sumner and sized down a few, like Fort Wingate, but the Defense Department expanded most others. In 1945, it created the White Sands Proving Ground near Alamogordo. During the war Kirtland had trained pilots for B-24 bombers, as well as crews and maintenance personnel. In 1945, the War Department renamed the Albuquerque Air Depot Station as Sandia Base and expanded its operations. And in 1963 the air force undertook an extensive expansion of Kirtland Base by establishing a related research laboratory. The new Kirtland Air Force Weapons Laboratory concentrated on developing advanced technologies that would aid the United States in staying ahead of the Soviet Union in weapons competition. The Defense Department undertook similar expansion at Cannon Air Force Base near Clovis. Its operations were closely related to a nationwide network developed by the Strategic Air Command, headquartered in Colorado Springs. As America's national-defense system after 1950 came to rely heavily on rockets and missiles, testing facilities for such weapons acquired an importance they had not had in previous years. Suddenly the wide, open spaces of western states like New Mexico took on new importance. By 1960 the Defense Department was greatly expanding the physical area of what had become the White Sands Missile Range near Alamogordo. Its large payroll made it the most significant employer in that part of the state.

The Cold War accelerated federal interest in scientific research related to the production of new weapons. Congress, in 1950, created the National Science Foundation, whose primary task was to dispense large sums to encourage the pursuit of science. It made the federal government the major patron of science in New Mexico, as in the United States. This was in stark contrast to the years before 1940, when sponsorship of scientific research was largely in the hands of private institutions, whether granted to universities or to individuals. New Mexico benefited from this federal largesse. Immediately after 1945, much debate took place within the Truman administration as to whether the laboratories at Los Alamos should be closed. After all, they had accomplished their mission. But the fears generated by the Cold War persuaded those who favored its continuation to develop additional atomic weapons. Thus, Los Alamos became established in New Mexico as one of the premier scientific laboratories in the United States. It left its imprint on the state by employing at least six thousand individuals annually and by attracting an able cadre of scientists.

Los Alamos also spawned other scientific projects throughout New Mexico. Most important were the Sandia Laboratories in Albuquerque, founded in 1947. Operated by the Westinghouse Corporation, Sandia employed between eight and ten thousand people annually. Many of its projects were related to national security, such as nuclear warheads, missiles, and lasers. During the 1950s it was also heavily involved with atomic testing in the Pacific area. Meanwhile, scientists working under federal grants at Alamogordo and White Sands were focusing more directly on research in rocketry and missiles, although after 1960 some programs were directed to space travel and to placing

Americans on the moon. Altogether, the federal science programs did a great deal to encourage scientific research in New
Mexico and provided it with a network of scientific installations such as it had not had before 1940.

Invariably, these programs resulted in an influx of newcomers to New Mexico. During the 1950s, it was reported,
Albuquerque had more Ph.D.s per capita than any other city in
the United States. Since Sandia Corporation then employed
about 10,000 people, these individuals with their families
constituted from 40,000 to 50,000 persons. No wonder the city
doubled its population from 100,000 in 1950 to twice that
number ten years later. In succeeding years the number of
Sandians was not always quite as high, but they constituted a
significant percentage of the total population. In the north, the
stabilization of the Los Alamos Laboratories led to the growth
of the city of Los Alamos. Before 1940 it had been a largely
unpopulated and isolated mesa (except for a boys' school). In a
state with a relatively small population like New Mexico, the
influx of people generated by federal science grants was of
crucial importance.

Apart from the Cold War, increased government expenditures affected the lives of New Mexicans and constituted a
second major influence on its development. Federal largesse
touched many spheres of New Mexico's growth. Since the
1930s federal programs in social welfare (such as social security)
directly impacted the state. As early as 1935 more than one-
third of New Mexico's people over sixty-five years of age were
mainly dependent on their social security payments, and in
succeeding years that percentage increased. When Congress,
under the leadership of Lyndon B. Johnson, enacted the Medi-
care and Medicaid acts of 1964 and 1965, it vastly expanded the
scope of such federal social programs, including not only old-
age pensions, but unemployment insurance, aid to dependent

children and the physically challenged, and special payments to single mothers. Federal monies also contributed importantly to the health care of New Mexicans. A substantial portion of the funds needed to establish the University of New Mexico Medical School in 1964 came from Congress. It was (and is, in 1992) the only medical school in the state. In succeeding years, federal grants continued to provide substantial support for its operation. And on Native American reservations, the Indian Health Service operated exclusively with federal monies.

During this period the federal government also entered into the field of education, which, before 1945, had been primarily a responsibility of state and local authorities. The program for free school lunches after 1965 affected a majority of the schoolchildren in the state. After 1965 federal college-loan programs touched a majority of college-bound students in New Mexico. Meanwhile, between 1965 and 1990 federal grants grew to an extent where they provided at least one-third of the budgets in some of the state's universities.

As a result of spin-offs from federal aid to social welfare and national defense programs, New Mexico businessmen and women built a fledgling electronics and biomedicals industry. Certainly, the state could not boast a Silicon Valley like California. But proximity to major laboratories stimulated the growth of a small network of such manufactures in New Mexico. By the 1970s the state's congressional delegations— especially U.S. Senator Pete Domenici—were actively engaged in developing institutionalized arrangements between the state's universities as well as with the laboratories and small-scale companies engaged in these newer industries.

Federal programs also affected the state's farmers. A myriad of federal farm programs embraced outright subsidies, low-cost loans, and disease-control policies that directly affected New Mexico farmers and cattle growers. A state like New Mexico,

A stretched-membrane heliostat at Sandia National Laboratories' Solar Thermal Test Facility is a key resource in the development of alternative energy. (Courtesy Sandia National Laboratories, neg. no. 0.8-2.3-18.6.)

where the federal government owned about one-third of the landed areas, could not help feeling the federal presence. Some of these lands were in public forests, while others were grazing areas, national parks, and monuments. Cattle growers as well as timber operators were often directly affected by particular federal grazing and timber policies.

But perhaps the scarcest natural resource in the West was water. New Mexicans were eager to enlist the help of the national government to develop and conserve their scarce water resources. In pursuance of that goal, substantial sums were invested by the Albuquerque District of the U.S. Army Corps of Engineers, the Bureau of Reclamation, and the U.S. Department of Agriculture. They improved navigation on the state's rivers, built dams at Cochiti and near Tucumcari, and undertook extensive flood-control programs throughout the state.

Federal programs affected many other aspects of the lives of New Mexicans as well. As a state with a large geographical area and a relatively small population, New Mexico before 1940 had been greatly burdened with building and maintaining public roads. That burden was eased with the Interstate Highway Act of 1956, when Congress poured large sums into the state to build its major arteries: Interstate Highway 40, running east to west, and Interstate Highway 25, going from north to south.

The federal government also spent substantial dollars in the development of energy sources. The Atomic Energy Commission, between 1946 and 1960, aided the construction of nuclear power plants in the Four Corners area. Its programs did much to invigorate the economy of that region, including Farmington and Durango (in Colorado).

A brief survey cannot do justice to the vast extent and influence of federal programs upon the lives of New Mexicans. But as even this cursory sketch has indicated, that impact is far reaching and profound. Without large-scale intervention by the federal government between 1940 and 1990, New Mexico—for better or for worse—would have had a very different pattern of development.

The third influence that shaped New Mexico's growth in the half-century after 1940 was technological change. In this brief sketch we can only hint at its ramifications. One example can suffice to serve as an illustration, however. Throughout its long history, New Mexico's growth was stunted by its isolation. Such isolation was greatly lessened by the enormous expansion of air travel after 1945, especially by the introduction of jets in

1960. That development did much to integrate New Mexico more closely into regional and national affairs. Not only did it shrink distances, but it alleviated a sense of psychological isolation that some New Mexicans had felt in earlier years. As in transportation, so in the realm of communication. The development of television in the 1950s did much to standardize popular culture in the United States. Even the most remote communities in New Mexico, including Indian reservations, were now exposed to television programming and became enmeshed in national trends, whether these affected values, tastes, dress, consumer goods, or entertainment. Television did much to homogenize many aspects of New Mexico's cultural life—to the dismay or delight of various segments of its population. Technological changes, therefore, were another major force in shaping New Mexico's destinies between 1940 and 1990.

Any discussion of the influences that shaped New Mexico's growth after 1940 cannot ignore a fourth factor, the unique characteristics of its environmental and geographical setting. The scenic beauty of the state made it a mecca for tourists. As one of the oldest settled areas in the United States, its historic sites—especially those encompassing ancient Native American and Hispanic cultures—added to its unique charm, which drew both tourists and new settlers. Paradoxically, its vast open spaces attracted not only those who sought the life of the spirit—such as the artists at Taos and Santa Fe—but the developers of destructive weapons who needed large tracts for testing.

New Mexico was also a storehouse for minerals. In 1950, as the Atomic Energy Commission developed nuclear facilities, Paddy Martínez, a Navajo sheepherder, discovered uranium near Grants, New Mexico. Until the discovery of the atomic bomb, there had been no demand for this mineral. But with the production of atomic weapons a new market arose, resulting in a short-lived mining boom. It collapsed by 1957, as the demand for uranium slackened. But the state also had other valuable minerals. The large copper deposits near Silver City continued to be productive, although changing world markets led to a gradual decline in copper production between 1970 and 1990. That was also true of the potash industry near Carlsbad after 1970. They became less productive and less competitive in the face of increasing global competition. In the north, coal mines near Raton prospered between 1960 and 1980. The demand for low sulfur coal increased during these years, when the power plants in the Four Corners area provided new and nearby markets. After 1980 they declined as opposition to nuclear power increased.

Petroleum producers in the state—near Hobbs and Farmington—had similar experiences. Meanwhile, New Mexico quietly became one of the nation's major producers of natural gas, as that energy source became important after 1950. The growth of new markets allowed New Mexico producers to export their gas—much of it produced in the Four Corners area—to the burgeoning new urban centers of the West Coast and the East. Throughout the years from 1950 to 1990, New Mexico ranked fourth or fifth nationally in total natural-gas production.

New Mexico's distinctive environmental setting enabled it to develop one of its most lucrative industries during this period—tourism. These years saw the opening of new ski resorts in Taos, Red River, Santa Fe, Albuquerque, and Ruidoso. State and national parks, such as Bandelier National Monument and White Sands National Monument as well as Carlsbad Caverns, became favorite destinations. Some of the Indian tribes took advantage of this new source of income. The Mescalero Apache tribe, for example, built the Sierra Blanca ski area in the Sacramento Mountains, and also a luxurious resort

Skiing in the mountains of New Mexico is a popular pastime particularly attractive to tourists. Photo by New Mexico Department of Development. (Courtesy Center for Southwest Research, General Library, University of New Mexico, neg. no. 000-158-0082.)

near Ruidoso. The Jicarilla Apache built a lodge at Stone Lake, in northwest New Mexico, to tap the new tourist market.

Of course, tourists were also attracted by New Mexico's distinctive culture. Santa Fe and Taos retained their aura as artistic centers. Although the famous artist Georgia O'Keeffe was reclusive, her home in Abiquiu strengthened New Mexico's image as an art center. At least five hundred new art galleries opened their doors in this period. Well-known painters, such as Peter Hurd in Roswell, and the Native American artist R. C. Gorman in Taos, as well as Pablita Velarde of Santa Clara

Pueblo, enhanced the state's reputation as an art center. After 1964 the Santa Fe Opera became world famous for its production of new works. It was the only regular outdoor opera house in the nation. The Santa Fe Chamber Music Festival, after 1980, and the establishment of the Desert Chorale there further strengthened the state's image as one of the cultural jewels in the United States and were required trips for sophisticated tourists.

Of course, the cultural background of New Mexico's people cannot be ignored as one of the formative influences in shaping its growth. From its beginnings, New Mexico has harbored a multicultural, pluralistic society that constituted a unique blend not found in any other state. The diverse cultures of its various Native American tribes provided one ingredient. The Hispanic heritage provided another. And the coming of diverse ethnic groups from other parts of the United States, between 1940 and 1990, provided still another component. These also included African-Americans, who had numbered only a handful in 1940, but came to constitute 2.3 percent of the population by 1990. The new economic opportunities in New Mexico between 1940 and 1990, as well as attractive climates and lifestyles, proved to be magnets that resulted in the most intensive expansion of population in its 3,500-year-old history. In 1940 the state had 530,000 people. By 1990 the census reported about 1.5 million, a threefold increase in just half a century. Much of that increase came in towns and cities.

Our sixth key to an understanding of the history of New Mexico between 1940 and 1990 is the affluence in the American economy, which also shaped New Mexico's experiences. Worldwide as well as in New Mexico, this was generally a period of economic expansion. World War II generated new consumer demands, while the postwar reconstruction of Germany and Japan also generated markets that began to decline by the 1970s. Some economists predicted that no similar boom could be

expected between 1989 and 2020 unless extraordinary conditions intervened. If New Mexico prospered during much of the
second half of the twentieth century, it was in part because
affluence came to be characteristic of a majority of Americans
after 1940. Reflections of this affluence have many implica-
tions for New Mexico, including the enormous increase of
population and a rising standard of living for many of its
inhabitants.

In this brief overview, we have focused on six keys to an
understanding of New Mexico's history from 1940 to 1990.
First, wars did much to shape the state's development—both
World War II and the Cold War. Second, government expenditures for a wide array of programs have played a decisive role.
Third, science and technology modified life in New Mexico, as
they did in much of the rest of the nation. Fourth, the geographical-environmental characteristics of the state have continued
to exert an influence on its development—even when modified
by technology. Fifth, New Mexico's unique amalgam of
peoples—old settlers and new—gave its society a distinctive
character. Sixth, the affluence that characterized American life
during much of this period undoubtedly affected New Mexico's
growth as well. Certainly, these six influences are not the only
ones that could be considered. But they do contribute to an
understanding of some of the dynamics that were responsible
for New Mexico's explosive growth in the half-century after
World War II.

BIBLIOGRAPHY

It is regrettable that students of New Mexico's history have
virtually ignored the twentieth century altogether. Detailed studies
of the sixteenth, seventeenth, eighteenth, and nineteenth centuries
abound, but the last one hundred years have been totally neglected.

Desperately needed is a volume that will provide a broad overview of this important period, the most significant in the state's long history, if growth and expansion are criteria. More specialized works detailing New Mexico's economic history, the development of its politics, its rich social fabric, its astounding cultural growth, and its environmental problems need to be written. In the absence of such works interested students are forced to grasp at bits and pieces.

A beginning inquiry into New Mexico's economic conditions can glean useful data from publications of the University of New Mexico's Bureau of Business Research and its successors. Helpful data are also found in Lance Chilton et al., *New Mexico: A Guide to the Colorful State* (Albuquerque: University of New Mexico Press, 1984). The book is an excellent compendium, chock-full of useful information. Brief background is provided by Leonard J. Arrington, "The New Deal in the West: A Preliminary Statistical Inquiry," *Pacific Historical Review* 38 (August 1969): 311–16. Here is an excellent brief article that places the post-World War II era in perspective. For the last decade, Lee Zink, *High Technology Industrial Development in New Mexico* (Albuquerque: University of New Mexico Press, 1982), is helpful.

The history of New Mexico politics is fragmented. Old, but suggestive, is Thomas C. Donnelly, ed., *Rocky Mountain Politics* (Albuquerque: University of New Mexico Press, 1940). Dean Donnelly, a former UNM faculty member, includes a good essay on New Mexico on the eve of the Second World War. F. Chris Garcia and Paul Hain, *New Mexico Government*, rev ed. (Albuquerque: University of New Mexico Press, 1981), contributes to an understanding of institutions. A brief list of relevant studies is noted in Frank H. Jonas, ed., *Bibliography on Western Politics: Selected, Annotated, with Introductory Essays* (Salt Lake City: Institute of Government, University of Utah, 1958), a supplement to *Western Political Quarterly* 11 (December 1958). Included in this book are a separate essay and a bibliography for each western state, including New Mexico. Jack E. Holmes, *Politics in New Mexico* (Albuquerque: University of New Mexico Press, 1967), is one of the few serious works on this important subject. Informal reminiscences are provided by Will A. Keleher, *New*

Mexicans I Knew: Memoirs 1892–1969 (Albuquerque: University of New Mexico Press, 1983). Suggestive materials are scattered in Clive S. Thomas, ed., *Politics and Public Policy in the Contemporary American West* (Albuquerque: University of New Mexico Press, 1991), an excellent array of articles on the American West, with some special attention to New Mexico. Broad background for the years before 1940 is provided by James T. Patterson, "The New Deal in the West," *Pacific Historical Review* 38 (August 1969): 317–27; and by Marc Simmons, *Albuquerque: A Narrative History* (Albuquerque: University of New Mexico Press, 1982). Although Simmons's book deals exclusively with years before 1940, it provides background. See also Simmons, *New Mexico*, rev ed. (Albuquerque: University of New Mexico Press, 1991).

Aspects of New Mexico's social history after 1940 have yet to be treated in a thorough fashion. Informative is Nancie L. González, *The Spanish-Americans of New Mexico: A Heritage of Pride*, rev. and enlarged ed. (Albuquerque: University of New Mexico Press, 1969), a fine guide to the social structure of New Mexico. Joseph V. Metzgar, "The Ethnic Sensibility of Spanish New Mexicans: A Survey and Analysis," *New Mexico Historical Review* 49 (January 1974): 49–73, is a helpful contribution. Manuel Servin, comp., *The Mexican-Americans: An Awakening Minority* (Beverly Hills, Calif.: Glencoe Press, 1970), does not concentrate on New Mexico, but is suggestive. Robert Kern, ed., *Labor in New Mexico: Unions, Strikes and Social History since 1881* (Albuquerque: University of New Mexico Press, 1983), provides a glimpse into the history of workers in the state. David Weber, ed., *Foreigners in Their Native Land: Historical Roots of the Mexican Americans* (Albuquerque: University of New Mexico Press, 1973), treats the entire Southwest, but refers to New Mexico as well. Richard M. Gardner, *¡Grito! Reies Tijerina and the New Mexico Land Grant War of 1967* (Indianapolis, Ind.: Bobbs-Merrill, 1970), deals with one of the more notable forms of social protest in this period.

General works on New Mexico's cultural heritage are lacking, although specialized studies on folklore, art, and architecture, as well as on literature, are informative; but they focus exclusively on the years before 1940, as does Ronald L. Davis, *A History of Opera in the American West* (Englewood Cliffs, N.J.: Prentice-Hall, 1965). This volume provides excellent background for understanding New Mexico's cultural scene. An extensive literature exists on Los Alamos and its history. A fine guide to it is found in Ferenc M. Szasz, *The Day the Sun Rose Twice: The Story of the Trinity Site Nuclear Explosion, July 16, 1945* (Albuquerque: University of New Mexico Press, 1984), one of the best works on the subject of science in New Mexico.

Apart from technical reports on various aspects of New Mexico's environment, little has yet been written on the historical dimensions of this topic. A brief account is Fred Irion, *New Mexico and Its Natural Resources 1900–2000* (Albuquerque: Division of Research, Department of Government, University of New Mexico, 1959), which is concise and informative. Workmanlike is U.S. Department of the Interior, *Natural Resources of New Mexico: "Land of Enchantment"* (Washington, D.C.: U.S. G.P.O., 1964). A well-written survey of one aspect is Michael Welsh, *A Mission in the Desert: Albuquerque District, 1935–1985* (Washington, D.C.: [U. S. Corps of Engineers,] 1985).

Clearly, the history of New Mexico after 1940 beckons to both young and old as an exciting field of study. If New Mexicans are to understand their heritage, if they are to have a clear sense of identity, and if its policymakers are to be guided by the experience of the past, then the present void needs to be filled by future generations.

TWO

TO GET ALONG OR
TO GO ALONG?

PLURALISTIC ACCOMMODATION VERSUS PROGRESS IN NEW MEXICO POLITICS AND GOVERNMENT

F. CHRIS GARCIA

INTRODUCTION

POLITICS and government in New Mexico are the topics of continual publicity and debate. Some observers have dubbed New Mexico "the political state" (Stumpf and Wolf, 1970) because politics have so thoroughly permeated the people, institutions, and social processes of the state. The political process and governmental activity is important in all of our states, but in New Mexico it seems to take on a particularly prominent and personal character. Politics seem to saturate every aspect of the state's activities, including its economics, and even its educational processes. The state's politics are at once pervasive and personal. Not only are all the state's citizens touched directly and frequently by political activities, but knowledge of who the political players are and personal relationships and acquaintances between them are important facets of New Mexicans' lives.

Why government and politics are so pervasive in New Mexico is open to much speculation. Perhaps it is, as Thomas Donnelly and others have hypothesized, because the sparse settlement and scarce economic resources of the state have magnified the importance of government. With such a vast, sparsely populated territory with minimal economic underpinnings, only government is able or willing to provide services, positions, and facilities that are not otherwise provided either by individuals or by the private sector. In this situation, not only are there greater expectations for government to provide social and welfare services, but government itself becomes an important economic and social player. For example, public-sector employment becomes a major source of jobs.

Perhaps the pervasiveness of politics is a result of New Mexico's historical experiences as an isolated colonial frontier of Spain and Mexico and also as a United States territory. As a Spanish frontier colony in the New World, this land was remote from its Hispanic government in Mexico and on the continent.

As a materially poor and undeveloped colony, it was highly dependent upon the proclamations and decrees of autocratic centralized governments in distant capitals. Although formally dependent on major decisions of a "foreign" government and subject to others that officials imposed upon them, residents of northern New Spain were ignored to an extent that required them to make day-to-day decisions themselves about the allocation of scarce resources; that is, engagement in local politics was necessitated. This situation existed for some two and a half centuries.

After the United States wrested this area from Mexico subsequent to its war with Mexico, New Mexico became a territory of the United States for sixty-four years. It still was a remote, isolated, and poor region, dependent upon a faraway sovereign—now the U.S. government—for its governors. It continued to be exploited for its resources, and even more so by the Americans than it had been by the Spanish and Mexicans. Entrepreneurs in and out of government made haste to use the newly imposed territorial government for purposes of the private exploitation of land, minerals, timber, water, and labor.

A premium was placed upon being involved in and skilled in politics. Many of the "natives" used politics as a defensive mechanism for their own communities. Others were successful in allying themselves with the economic and political interests who were after private gain. Some used politics to curry favor with the powerful interests.

In sum, politics as a "web of favor and obligation" developed as an important mode of social accommodation over three centuries. Politics was paramount. Government, and especially its institutions, was of secondary concern to the conflict-resolving, resource-allocating political process.

New Mexico government in its current constitutional configuration is relatively young, dating back to the state's constitution, drawn up in 1910, and to statehood, in 1912. New Mexico entered the union as a preindustrial state with a preindustrial economy. Even though a young state, it brought with it a legacy, including a political culture, of three centuries of distant, authoritarian government and pervasive politics, especially local politics. The eighty years of statehood is a relatively short time as governments go. Yet in these eight decades there have been tremendous changes in American society. Advances in the technologies of communication, information, and transportation, as well as scientific breakthroughs, have greatly altered the lives of people during that time period. There also have been major economic changes, particularly the emergence of the modern welfare state, with the national government assuming the role of guarantor, if not provider, of social services since the "New Deal" era of sixty years ago. Particularly since World War II, the federal government has had a tremendous impact on New Mexico. Its presence is pervasive. Much of the economy is dependent on federal spending through the two national research and development laboratories, several defense installations, and many social-service programs. In the 1990s, New Mexico received more dollars than the state paid in federal taxes and fees. Indeed, the state was second among all states in the proportion of federal dollars it received compared to its contributions to the federal treasury.

Socially, the demographic composition of our society has witnessed major changes. There has been a huge influx of persons from other states and countries attracted to the Land of Enchantment since World War II. Much urbanization has occurred, as both the new residents and those previously living in the rural areas and small towns of the state moved to the larger metropolitan areas of Albuquerque, Santa Fe, and Las Cruces.

Our focus in this essay will be to examine whether and, if so, how these major changes outside the political system have affected the politics and government of New Mexico. The focus is on the years following World War II, when changes in New Mexican society greatly accelerated. The primary observation to be made is that while there have been changes in the politics and governmental processes of New Mexico, these have been minimal and incremental when measured against the vast and rapid changes taking place in the economic, technological, and social spheres. The basic pattern of politics in New Mexico and its major constitutional structures remain little changed over the past fifty years. Consequently, New Mexico government is becoming increasingly out of sync with changes occurring in other areas. With the political process and government itself becoming more distant from the people, it is not serving the general citizenry as well, and indeed now is minimally responsive and responsible to the people in the state. This minimal responsiveness has reached the point of a near critical situation, a point that calls for major and fundamental, including constitutional, reforms. Indeed, early in 1992, Governor Bruce King— certainly not known as a radical reformer, but certainly possessing as much experience in high levels of New Mexico government as anyone else—called for some major amendments to the constitution. Additionally, a bill was introduced in the 1992 session of the legislature that would fund a commission to study the possible revision of this "antiquated document."

New Mexico's government has lagged behind in its adaptation to the changes of the modern era for a variety of reasons. Typically, many of our societal institutions often do respond to, rather than precede, social transformations. In fact, in the United States as a whole, the political culture has traditionally preferred that government be a reactive rather than a proactive institution. Be that as it may, in New Mexico the unresponsiveness problem seems to be particularly pronounced and regressive.

A major reason that New Mexico has lagged behind even most other states in its adaptation to changing conditions is one that is peculiar to New Mexico. It is a condition that paradoxically could be judged a success by another set of standards. This is the continual accommodation of the diversity of distinctive interests, particularly regional and cultural interests. Observers have long noted that the state is distinctive because it consists of regionally and culturally distinct political subcultures. For example, that perceptive scholar of New Mexico politics, Thomas C. Donnelly, writing about the state in 1940, entitled his piece "New Mexico: An Area of Conflicting Cultures."

Since 1848, when New Mexico became a U.S. territory as a result of the U.S. conquest of Mexico, to the current time, there has been an underlying tension between the native peoples of the area and the U.S. "Anglos." This has been a dominant, if downplayed, theme throughout the state's history. There has been a continual and constant effort to maintain harmonious relationships between at least the three major cultural groups in the state—the Hispanics, the Indians, and the Anglos. At times, this tension has surfaced, sometimes even manifesting itself in violence. But, by and large, the history of relations among these groups in this state has been one of "peaceful coexistence." Indeed, New Mexico is sometimes held up as a shining example of successful cultural *pluralism*, that is, a society in which distinctive cultural groups, while maintaining their identities, exist in a relatively peaceful atmosphere of tolerance, even mutual respect, and cooperation.

This accommodation of our distinctive cultures has taken place both inside and outside politics. However, the political arena has been one of the major places in which such cultural accommodation has taken place. Politics, after all, has as its essence the resolution of conflicts and the competition among individuals and groups to secure government support for their own positions. As a major means of conflict resolution, politics in New Mexico has been a singularly important process through which conflicting needs, both symbolic and material, among our various ethnic groups have been resolved. This process of political accommodation should be noted and commended for its success. However, the attention, energy, and resources that have gone into the internal processes of mutual adjustment and accommodation have diverted these resources from other political and government objectives or achievements.

The overarching thesis of this essay, therefore, is that the minimal and piecemeal responsiveness of New Mexico government to many of the pressing problems of the state is at least partially the result of the predominance of the politics of cultural accommodation within the state. Such a high price is paid for the accommodation, if not the integration, of our political subcultures, that few resources are left for government to be responsive to the needs of the people of this state as a whole, the New Mexico commonwealth.

This cultural accommodation has manifested itself politically in very conservative and cautious government and politics, in which experimentation, innovation, and leadership take a backseat to the muting of conflict. The changes that do occur are incremental, and the system responds only enough to meet the pressure put on it and thus vitiate any impending crisis. The system is carefully and cautiously *balanced* in many ways. Power is divided among many segments, and the whole system is balanced among these competing players. For example, no one individual or group can emerge by taking a high profile or by exerting leadership lest the system become unbalanced and the ever-present centrifugal forces of regional cultures shatter the state's cultural mosaic. Government policies and other "payoffs" are incremental and scattered; all major political players get a little something; none are completely excluded.

More specifically, the patterns in New Mexico politics over the past half century include:

- a cautious, conservative, wary approach to government as a problem solver;
- a resistance to change and a reluctance to act in any major innovative way that might upset the existing *balance*;
- an incremental, piecemeal, fragmented approach to policymaking;
- policymaking characterized by "a little bit for (almost) everyone";
- a marked *localism*, with a corresponding lack of concern for the state as a whole polity;
- a shortage of vision and of long-range planning, and an overly narrow and short-term perspective;
- more responsiveness to particularistic and parochial interests—individuals, interest groups, and regions—than to the general citizenry;
- an overriding concern with balancing the major economic and regional-cultural interests;
- a shortage of statewide leadership, perhaps even an oppo-

sition to any one individual or any one group attempting to exert leadership;

• overall, an entrenched collection of status-quo interests supported by an outdated constitution and a distrustful and fragmented political culture.

Therefore, the major achievement of the political system is that it has been able to persist by successfully accommodating to significant internal diversity. However, paradoxically, this success may also have pre-empted the system's capacity to address other critical problems and pressures that reflect the social and economic changes of the past half-century. By the measure of resolving internal conflicts, New Mexico government and politics can be judged a success. Measured by its responsiveness to most other problems of the modern era, it is perilously close to being a failure. With the ever-increasing pressures of the modern era, New Mexico government and politics are themselves increasingly out of sync. Reforms to make them more responsive to the public's needs and more responsible to the state's citizenry are badly needed.

Resistant as they are, even New Mexico's government and politics have incurred some change over the past fifty years. Most of it has occurred grudgingly or haphazardly. And the patterns of change, and more clearly the lack thereof, illustrate the theme and specific variations on it, presented above.

PATTERNS AND TRENDS

One cannot fail to be impressed by the very minimal changes that have occurred in New Mexico government over the past fifty years, in marked contrast to the continuity of basic political patterns; and perhaps one may even be amazed at how major reform has been avoided. In the following presentation, some of the changes that have occurred in our political processes and governmental institutions over the past fifty years will be reviewed. An examination of these will reveal the themes suggested above, plus more specific related trends.

THE CONSTITUTION   The basic document on which New Mexico government is based is the state's constitution. This was drawn up by a Constitutional Convention in 1910 in conjunction with the state's submission for statehood status. The convention was comprised of a relatively diverse group of the state's citizenry, with the notable exceptions of Indians and women. Most major regional, cultural, and economic interests were in attendance, including a substantial representation of Hispanics. This was a conservative group of convention delegates, seemingly isolated from the progressive movements occurring in the rest of the nation. Even though the Progressive and Populist movements were very strong in some parts of the United States, they seemed to have little impact on this convention. The basic document was modeled after that of the U.S. Constitution, although it was more than three times as long, considerably more detailed, and, if possible, more conservative, protecting the interests of the elite of those times. Some of the considerations uppermost in the delegates' minds were to protect and preserve the status-quo interests and to maintain that balance of interests that had developed and been maintained over the preceding half-century as a territory. Government was to be minimized, and that which was created was to be fractionalized and constrained. Constitutional power was fragmented even to a greater degree than in the United States Constitution. For example, a multimember collective executive was established (about which more will be said later). The people (more specifically, the dominant interests) were to be protected from state government, and the state government was to be distanced from the people. Local, regional, and cultural interests retained control. Although certain traditional rights of Hispanics were reinforced, Native Americans were not even provided with the franchise.

The document is a conservative one and is highly resistant to change. Not only is it difficult to amend the constitution of this state, but there are provisions, particularly with regard to the rights of Hispanics, for which amendments are so difficult that they are deemed "unamendable." Partisanship was a strong factor in the actions of the delegates, more important than the considerations of responsibility, responsiveness, effectiveness, and questions of ideology. Indeed, perhaps the only commonly shared ideology was that of conservatism and elitism, that is, the exclusion of the people from direct participation. In this latter regard, there were no provisions for the popular recall of public officials, nor were there provisions for a popular initiative regarding legislation; both were progressive ideas being added, at that time, to many western state constitutions. It was to be the elected representatives who could initiate legislation and who could remove others from office through impeachment. The people were given only limited powers of direct action—for example, through referenda, that is, the capacity to vote on proposed changes to the constitution, by voting on amendments proposed and passed by the legislature. Even then, numerical and regional minorities are given a veto power.

So the basic document of the state reflects the accommodation and balancing of the economic and cultural interests of the time. It scattered power into many areas and evidenced a distrust of direct popular participation in most segments of society, thereby making concerted or directed governmental action all but impossible. It encouraged the processes of negotiation and compromise and all but guaranteed that change would be incremental, if at all, and always difficult.

THE LEGISLATURE   Recent survey research on the opinions of the state's citizens reveals the public's very low level of confidence in the New Mexico state legislature. That branch is held in even lower esteem than other state public agencies. This seems to have changed relatively little over the past fifty years. Donnelly noted, in the late 1940s, that "people no longer have faith and confidence in the state legislature"(53). In keeping with the pattern established by the nation's founding fathers, a bicameral legislature was established for New Mexico. The Senate represented counties, and the somewhat larger House of Representatives was based on districts that themselves were county based. Initially, the legislature had been small, with 24 senators and 49 members of the House. The trend over the years has been toward increasing the size of the legislature. In 1949, there were 31 members in the Senate and 55 in the House. Today, the legislature is comprised of 112 members—70 members of the House of Representatives and 42 senators.

Through the 1950s and 1960s the legislature was disproportionately representative of rural areas and small towns. People in Bernalillo County had as little as one-forty-eighth of the representation in rural counties. In the "reapportionment revolution" of the 1960s, the federal courts required equal representation along "one-person, one-vote" lines. The legislature resisted this change and the possible shifts in traditional power that reapportionment could portend. Its minimal, conservative, and incremental reapportionment plans were rejected by the federal courts in 1964, 1966, and following each of the 1970, 1980, and 1990 censuses. One result was the expansion of the size of the legislature in 1966 and 1970. In order to protect incumbents and their interests, additional districts have been added rather than seriously revising the fewer extant districts.

Although fifty years ago Anglos were the overwhelming majority in the Senate, Hispanics in the House did have a

Legislators debate bills at the capitol in Santa Fe. Photo by Neil Jacobs. (Courtesy Office of Secretary of State.)

sizeable minority. This cultural accommodation evidenced in the House became increasingly reflected in the Senate after the reapportionment revolution of the 1960s and 1970s. Currently, the major cultural groups are represented in both houses at or slightly below their proportion of the population. A few women have gained membership in the legislature, but they are still grossly underrepresented.

The public's past and present distrust of legislators is reflected in the many restrictions placed (and retained) on their power. Perhaps the major ones are the limitations on sessions and salaries. In a pattern that has persisted from statehood, the legislature meets for only relatively short periods of time. Until 1966, the legislature met only every two years for sixty days. Currently, it meets annually, but only in short, thirty-day

sessions on even-numbered years and for sixty days in odd-
numbered years. Legislators are not salaried but, instead, re-
ceive minimal per-diem expenses. The citizens of the state
seem to feel that by not paying the legislators they will make
the members "citizen legislators" rather than professionals.
The citizenry seems to prefer a legislature that is relatively
amateurish, hoping that this will mean they are closer to the
grass roots.

Yet these restrictions do impose handicaps on the legislators. For instance, expertise and resources for dealing with the
problems presented to the legislature must be found, and they
have been provided largely by lobbyists. Lobbyists representing
organized interests have proliferated over the past five decades.
Early on, they were fewer and reflected primarily agricultural,
livestock, mining, educational, and ethnic interests. Now there
is a much greater diversity of representation of various interests
throughout the state, including businesses, the educational
sector, other public-sector agencies, retail and wholesale organizations, trade and professional organizations, environmental
groups, and many others. Control and regulation of these
special interests is weak, as the state has maintained only
minimal lobbyist registration and contribution disclosure laws
over the course of its history.

There have been several attempts to pay the legislators
salaries, in addition to per diem. Some of these have been driven
by hopes that paying salaries would make legislators less
dependent upon the lobbyists for resources and also by the hope
that it would diversify the economic bases of the representatives, bringing in more blue-collar and wage-earner representatives. However, every attempt to enact legislative salaries has
been defeated. Proposals to increase the length of sessions or to
have unlimited sessions have also gone down to defeat.

Areas in which some professionalization has occurred

include the building of legislative staff, such as the Legislative Council Service, which can and does provide technical and legal expertise to the legislators. Also, there has developed over the past twenty years a great dependence on interim committees, which meet between sessions to prepare for the limited plenary sessions. These were part of the legislative reforms of the 1950s and 1960s, perhaps the zenith of state legislative power and performance. During those decades, a combination of piece-meal constitutional amendments and internal reorganizations resulted in annual sessions, standing committees, a legislative council and legislative council service, and interim commit-tees. These reforms, long overdue, along with a well-equipped new capitol building, brought nationwide recognition and new optimism that the people's representatives would catch up with the conditions of an increasingly complex society.

Institutional reform has not brought policy innovation or even improved responsiveness to the state's needs. The New Mexico legislature continues to be a very personalistic, inter-nally oriented, and reactive body. Providing "casework service" to its constituents, mainly by doing favors for friends and influential interests; reacting to the most powerful pressures brought upon it; being primarily concerned with its own busi-ness; and serving, by and large, as a status quo reinforcing instrument characterize the legislature. Many legislators seem to be there either only to advance their own individual interests or to protect the interests of their most important constituents. There seems to be little organized or coordinated effort to address comprehensively the many problems facing contempo-rary New Mexicans. Problems in the economy, child care, health care, social services, criminal justice, education, and the deteriorating infrastructure are minimally addressed. Some-times it seems only enough action is taken to stave off a crisis.

In spite of a few institutional changes, there seems to have been little improvement or change in the character, style, or products of the legislature over the past half-century. Writing fifty years ago, Thomas Donnelly was very critical of the legislature and expressed hope for its reform and improvement. He stated that "a democratic and representative government needs an efficient functioning legislature to keep it strong and effective in dealing with the complex problems of modern statehood" (112). A half-century later, the situation is relatively unchanged. Suggestions for reform include making the legislature a smaller, perhaps unicameral, body that is salaried with unlimited terms of two or four years and that would meet in annual sessions with no prescribed limit. Along with this would go improved regulation of the many interest groups that are rampant in the decision-making activities of the legislature.

Although one cannot give the legislature high marks as an institution that can or will provide progressive policies and leadership in the areas of social justice and promote the general welfare, it may be simply reflecting, as a microcosm, the fragmented political culture from which it comes. Perhaps its latent function of cultural and regional accommodations is being served well through its resolution of conflict through continual negotiation, compromising, horse trading, and wheeling-dealing. A quarter of a century ago, a scholar and admirer of the legislature, Jack Holmes, insightfully commented that "[the legislature's] inclination to create its own culture and minuscule internal republic may make the legislature an instrument highly useful in containing and converting to a satisfactory social product the forces at work in the larger society of New Mexico, which . . . is inherently neither polity nor community" (284).

In the meantime, although the internal accommodation of interests will continue to be maintained, there seems to be little chance of leadership and progress emerging from the legislature. New Mexicans, lacking confidence in the legislature's ability to meet its challenges, may have to look elsewhere for effective leadership and problem solving. It is to one such possibility, the executive branch, to which we now turn.

THE EXECUTIVE   If the New Mexico citizenry looks for alternative sources of leadership in the state's executive branch, it is likely to be disappointed. The executive branch is constitutionally and politically fragmented; and the "first among equals," the governor, is himself severely constrained. At the national level, the chief executive, the president, has increasingly exerted dominance in the nation's public affairs over the legislature. In New Mexico, this has not been the case. In fact, if anything, over the past fifty years the governor has become less involved in policy leadership vis-à-vis the legislature.

We have seen that to accommodate the strong cultural and regional diversity within the state, the constitution fragmented governmental power. It did this not only between branches through the federal analogy of separation of powers, but in New Mexico also within the executive branch itself. In addition to the governor, eight other state executives were to be independently and directly elected by the people. The governor was left, at best, the first among equals with other executive powers assigned to the attorney general, the secretary of state, the state auditor, the state treasurer, the commissioner of public lands, the state superintendent of public instruction, and the three-member state corporation commission. The lieutenant governor was also independently elected, although independently exercising few executive powers. Fred Irion observed, in 1956, that "each of these elective executives represents a center of political power." This "collective executive" is still largely in place, although New Mexicans no longer elect the state school superintendent.

New Mexico State Supreme Court Justices (from left to right): Seth Montgomery, Richard E. Ransom, Dan Sosa, Joseph F. Baca, and Gene Franchini. (Courtesy Office of Secretary of State.)

The trends in the office of the governor have been toward slightly decreased power vis-à-vis the legislature and increased power in the administrative area. One thereby could argue, with some justification, that the power of the governor has remained at about the same level even though its base has changed. Prior to World War II and up into the 1950s, the bases of the governor's power were twofold—the leadership of his political party and his appointment power, or the power of patronage. Candidates for governor typically worked their way up through the ranks of the party, seeking various appointed and elected offices. All of the men who were governors in the first half-century of statehood had previous experience in state politics before becoming governor. Most of them had served in lesser state and local offices for several years before seeking the top post.

New Mexico lacked a comprehensive merit system and civil service until the early 1960s. Since virtually all public offices could be filled on the basis of partisan appointments by the governor, this gave him great leverage both within his political party and within state government. The civil service reforms of the 1960s, however much they diminished nepotism and patronage and increased objectivity and professionalism, certainly undermined the traditional base of influence of the New Mexico governor. Although political parties were still fairly cohesive and disciplined in New Mexico until the 1950s or 1960s, this common party loyalty also helped to hold together the plural executive, as typically all of the state's elected executives were members of the same party. However, the advent of modern campaign techniques, which rely more upon nonpartisan and professional campaign managers, pollsters, image-makers, and technicians, greatly weakened the political parties in New Mexico. Having lost much of his power base in the party and patronage systems, the governor's potential for leadership, especially concerning the legislature, was weakened.

The reason that one could reasonably claim that the governor of contemporary New Mexico is at relatively the same level of power as in the 1940s and 1950s is that a new basis for support has been found. Donnelly observed that New Mexicans had always evidenced a strong desire for personal leadership and that "a flair for the dramatic is also a helpful asset in any candidate as the public prefers its leaders to be good showmen" (114). Much of the focus of the contemporary media on New Mexico government spotlights the governor. The citizenry has a much easier time focusing upon government when it can personalize it, especially in the form of one individual. In New Mexico, as in most systems, that individual will be the chief executive. The plural executive and the legislature notwithstanding, New Mexicans tend (perhaps unfairly) to place the burdens of leadership on the New Mexico governor, and largely because of the personalization of government, which is enhanced by the media.

Today, as over the past fifty years, the office of the governor commands more public respect by far than does the legislature. Yet the governor has less political power than he did previously. However, any governor who wishes to can attempt to exert more or less leadership in the position. His own personality, philosophy, and desires do affect his leadership role in the system.

As a result of these foregoing factors, most New Mexico governors have carried on the tradition of "weak" governors rather than exerting strong and directive leadership in the position. Not only is the institutional structure of the state such that the governor's powers are severely limited, New Mexicans actually seem to prefer a ceremonial statesman rather than a policy leader in the office of the governor. For example, for most of New Mexico's history governors were limited to two terms of two years each. Proposals for four-year terms were defeated in 1927 and 1948. Finally, in 1970, the voters accepted a constitutional amendment for a single four-year term. However, neither the governor nor any other state executive, excluding the lieutenant governor, could follow with another four-year term in any of the state-elected offices. The possibility of two successive, four-year terms for all the state executives was realized in 1988. This was out of character not only with the tradition of New Mexicans, but also with other electoral results of that general election, and it led some to believe that it was a "mistake" caused by the ambiguity in the language of the constitutional amendment.

This ambivalence between expecting leadership from the governor and not actually wanting him to exercise any power has molded the modern governorship in New Mexico. One could contrast the popular administrations of Garrey Carruthers and Bruce King with the less popular administrations of Jerry Apodaca and Toney Anaya. One element in the different ways they were received by the population is that King and Carruthers emphasized the ceremonial and symbolic "chief-of-state" functions of the position. King, in particular, was skilled at the politics of accommodation, negotiation, and compromise honed by his previous service in the state legislature. Carruthers was more charismatic and media oriented. On the other hand, Apodaca and, to a greater extent, Anaya attempted to provide policy initiatives and leadership and sometimes acted in a decisive and directive manner, a style that proved to be not very acceptable or successful in this state.

A historical footnote that illustrates some of the ethnic accommodation in executive politics involves the ethnic "ticket balancing" for the governor and lieutenant-governor positions. For decades, as Donnelly has noted, the political parties did everything possible to make sure that Anglos would run against Anglos and Hispanics against Hispanics as a way of muting conflict; and this was reflected, for example, in the congressional representation for New Mexico. Through most of its history, New Mexico has had one Anglo senator and one Hispanic senator; one Anglo representative and one Hispanic representative in Congress. Moreover, traditionally, the gubernatorial nominee for each party was an Anglo, and this was balanced by a Hispanic lieutenant governor. These ethnic assignments were traditional until the 1960s, when the control of party caucuses and conventions weakened and primaries became dominant. Since then, in some cases, the top spot has gone to Hispanics, and sometimes both positions have been filled by Anglos. In 1990, the election of Bruce King as governor and Casey Luna as lieutenant governor once again manifested the traditional balancing act. The Republicans balanced their gubernatorial nominee, Frank Bond, with the first female nominated for lieutenant governor, Mary Thompson.

THE (OTHER COLLECTIVE) EXECUTIVES   New Mexico's collective executives, consisting of several positions that are subject to direct election by a statewide constituency,

Stephanie Gonzales, New Mexico's twentieth Secretary of State, is the most recent in a long line of women to hold that office. Photo by Linda Montoya. (Courtesy Office of Secretary of State.)

do not help in fixing responsibility nor in promoting leadership. However, such fragmentation does serve the tradition of accommodation and of giving all major interests a little piece of the action. Throughout New Mexico's history, but particularly since World War II, there have been proposals by reformers to consolidate many or most of the executive offices into one office under the direction of the governor, or at least to cut back somewhat on the number of independently elected executives. Recommendations for focusing executive responsibility came forth in a major way, in 1952, with the recommendations of the Governor's Committee on Reorganization of the Executive Branch, or the "Little Hoover" committee. The committee recommended that several of the elected executive offices be eliminated and made subject to appointment by the governor, and it also advocated that the tremendous proliferation of independent and uncoordinated state agencies be consolidated. The recommendations were duly accepted and duly ignored. In referring to this 1952 attempt in 1956, Irion tried to explain "why modern means of administration have been shunned so often in New Mexico," and he suggested that "perhaps the explanation is partly a matter of psychology" (48). It surely does reflect the fragmented political culture of the state. New Mexico's 1969 Constitutional Convention also called for a consolidation of the plural executive and a decrease in number of "a horde of conflicting overlapping uncoordinated agencies." This proposal, along with other proposed governmental reforms, was rejected by the people. Later, the Governor's Committee on Executive Reorganization under Jerry Apodaca recommended major consolidation among the literally hundreds of agencies, boards, and commissions that were only nominally a part of the state's executive branch.

As reported by Dorothy Cline, under Jerry Apodaca's governorship, a successful consolidation did occur with as many as two hundred agencies reordered into twelve major cabinet departments, with one each headed by a secretary appointed by the governor. As much as this was a major accomplishment, the constitutionally based plural-executive structure outside of the governor's control was not tackled by this reorganization. However, even this much-needed and long-overdue consolidation of some agencies led Dorothy Cline to claim hopefully that "for a first time since statehood, the governor of New Mexico became in fact the chief executive of a substantial portion of the executive establishment." Although this consolidation helped, New Mexico's plural executive remains an example of the fragmentation of power that precludes the fixing of responsible leadership and reflects the process of duplicating policies or positions for every independent interest.

THE JUDICIARY   In the United States, the judiciary has been described as the "less-political" branch. This is less the case in New Mexico, where the politics of accommodation, compromise, and decentralization have been manifested in the judicial branch. Throughout the first several decades of our history, the New Mexico judiciary was as political as the other branches. Although the court structure paralleled that of the federal system—with levels consisting of trial courts of the first instance, courts of appeal, and, ultimately, a supreme court, the methods of selection and qualifications were distinctive. Through the 1940s, 1950s, and 1960s, all judges in the state were elected, and they were elected on a partisan basis. Judicial qualifications, particularly at the lowest level—the justice of the peace—were nonexistent or minimal. In fact, the allocation of justice-of-the-peace and magistrate positions to virtually every small community in the state was viewed as a distribution throughout the state of some of the many political plums involving government employment and payrolls. Writing in the early 1950s, Thomas Donnelly stated that "it appeared the system will remain unchanged for some time to come" (284). The system persisted for another two decades, until a reorganization of the structure did take place. The system of judicial selection was drastically changed in 1988. In resolution of the debate about whether the state's judges should be elected or appointed, there was devised an arcane and eclectic (but perhaps typically New Mexican) system of initial recommendation by a "blue-ribbon" commission, followed by appointment by the governor, then followed by a partisan election, and finally followed by a nonpartisan retention election. This complicated procedure is symbolic of New Mexico's politics of trying to give everybody a little bit of something and of not being decisive in any one direction.

Although most interests were once again accommodated, it is interesting to note that women in New Mexico were

Innovative voting machines allow easy access for all voters. (Courtesy Office of Secretary of State, neg. no. 81-A.)

debarred from trial juries until 1951. Just as there are disproportionately few women in the legislature and in the executive branch, there are correspondingly low numbers of women in judicial positions.

LOCAL GOVERNMENTS   There are two or three points to be made about local governments in New Mexico, observations that reflect the themes of accommodation, conservatism, and incrementalism. There are probably many times more units of local government than there ought to be, ideally, from a standpoint of efficiency. Since statehood, county governments have increased in number even though population movements toward concentrations in urban areas have left many counties with scarcely any population and with a minimal infrastructure of services.

The same is true of many school districts. Among the eighty-eight currently operating in New Mexico, several are barely able to function because of their very small population and resource bases. But consolidation is strenuously opposed. Actually, even though there may be too many school districts, it is revealing that this, in itself, is a product of reform because at one time the state had more than five hundred school districts, which included county school systems, interstate school districts, rural school districts, municipal school districts, and independent rural districts.

Whereas it might make logical sense to consolidate city and county governments, particularly in urban counties such as Bernalillo County, attempts to do so have failed, since they require the separate approval of county residents residing outside the city limits. County governments in New Mexico, as in most other places, are known for their minimal level of efficiency and effectiveness in carrying out governmental responsibilities as well as for being important in providing employment opportunities and government business for favored individuals and interests. The 1992 legislature passed a law that would allow a substantial portion of Bernalillo County to split off and become New Mexico's thirty-fourth county. Once again, the strong localism and defensiveness of the political culture was evidenced in "state" politics.

Although New Mexico has gone from a largely rural to a largely urban state in the past fifty years, this shift has hardly been reflected in its local governments. Most village, town, and city governments are as they were forty or fifty years ago. Some professionalization has occurred, primarily in the more populous counties, and through the incorporation of professional "managers," for example.

In spite of the few reforms that have occurred, it is clear that there are still far too many local governments to allow for efficient and effective provision of public services, particularly given the weak economic base of the state. Yet "access," the availability of jobs, personal relationships with government officials, and the defense of local-cultural interests have persisted in place of effectively meeting the public's policy needs.

VOTING, ELECTIONS, AND POLITICAL PARTIES

For the first forty years of its history, New Mexico had a strong political party system and a high-to-average level of participation by voters in elections. For the first half of New Mexico's history as a state, political parties were strong, disciplined, and quite closed to new elements or changes. Since World War II the political parties have been "strong" only in keeping the organizations together, primarily for the purpose of serving the interests of the activists and not in providing cohesive packages of policy alternatives to the voters. Jack Holmes observed that as the party balance shifted to the Democrats and as both parties declined in strength, "increasingly diverse regional and group differences became more critically sensitive . . . " (220). As parties continued to decline in the mid-1950s, they were criticized for not offering meaningful alternatives to the voters; at that time, however, the hope was expressed that "as the cultural patterns of the state change in response to the impact of the mid-twentieth century, this [would] change" (Irion and Judah, 22). In the 1990s no noticeable improvement has occurred, and hope is waning.

Yet social and economic changes during the past fifty years have caused some major changes in the political parties, in voting, and in elections, and perhaps more than they have stirred changes in our governmental institutions.

Most of the time since World War II, and actually beginning

with the New Deal, New Mexico was classified as a "modified, one-party (Democratic) state." Registration was heavily Democratic, averaging a ratio of about two Democrats to one Republican, and most of the officials elected were Democrats. However, in the two decades before the New Deal, the state was largely Republican among both the Anglo and Hispanic populations. After the New Deal, and persisting until quite recently, the urban areas of the state and the Anglos were predominantly Republican. The rural areas of north-central New Mexico and the eastern, or "Little Texas," counties were largely Democratic. Over the last three decades, the Hispanic population has become increasingly Democratic while the Anglo population, including the previously Democratic areas of "Little Texas," has become more Republican, as evidenced by the voting for the top of the ticket. Party and ethnicity have become more congruent as the relative size of the Hispanic population has diminished. The voters in the east side of the state, always more conservative in their cultural orientations, have become more Republican. The ratio between the two parties has changed. The Democrats retain a majority party in registration, but it is an increasingly smaller one—approximately 1.7 to 1 in 1992.

Regarding voter participation, the problem in the past was sometimes not so much that there was not enough participation in voting, but too much, as sometimes voters exceeded the number of those in the population actually eligible to vote! In fact, it was only during the prewar period that New Mexicans voted in higher than average numbers. Statewide electoral turnouts since the 1950s have ranged from low to average when compared to the national means. The relationship of this pattern to that of the decline in political parties and the replacement of the power of the party nominating conventions by the direct primary is more than coincidental.

New Mexico is one of the few places where Hispanics have

participated in political party activities and elections at a rate equal to or sometimes greater than that of Anglos. Voting information about elections during the 1970s and 1980s show that the voting rate for Hispanics and Anglos is very comparable now. Moreover, the overall participation rate in elections has decreased, becoming more similar to the national average rather than well above it, as it was in earlier decades. One should note that Native Americans participate only minimally in the nontribal political system, partly because Indians living on reservations were denied the franchise in state elections until 1948. However, the rate of participation has been growing. As an example of such increased involvement, seven Native Americans were serving in the state legislature in 1992.

There has been some democratization among the state's political parties during the decades preceding and following World War II. Previously, party affairs were very closed to newcomers. Nominees for office were selected in closed sessions, either by caucus by or closed party conventions. The closed primaries did replace the convention system in 1938, much to the disgruntlement of party activists. In 1948, the primary system was modified by having a preprimary convention that certified party recommendations to participate in the primary. Later, the nomination system was again changed to eliminate the preprimary convention. Another indication of this exclusivity, or fear of new elements, is that no absentee voting was allowed in the state until 1952.

Campaigns and elections have been relatively unregulated by the state. Although calls for campaign-expenditure reforms, including limitations and disclosures, have been heard over the past several decades, New Mexico still has some of the loosest regulations and laws of any state in the nation.

One other noteworthy difficulty that remains is the long or "bedsheet" ballot. New Mexico is one of the few states that has persisted in electing scores of public officials. The plural executive, elected judges, and the several elected statewide boards and commissions, such as the Corporation Commission and the State Board of Education, are illustrative of just a few of the offices for which New Mexicans must select occupants. Typically, the voter is faced with a ballot containing an overwhelming and bewildering array of positions, candidates, offices, bond issues, and propositions. In the 1990 general election, there were more than sixty-five items about which the voter was asked to make decisions! This certainly reflects, among other things, the historical distrust of government and the "a-little-bit-for-everyone" style of New Mexico politics.

OVERVIEW AND OBSERVATIONS

We have reviewed some of the changes that have occurred in our governmental institutions and political processes in New Mexico during the past half-century. If there have been patterns or trends, they are not clearly distinguishable, primarily because the changes have been surprisingly minimal. In fact, this in itself may be the major pattern; that is, government has changed only incrementally to meet minimally the increasing pressures on it that have been brought about by the tremendous changes in the economic, scientific, technological, and social makeup of our state. New Mexico still is operating basically with the same constitutional system devised eighty years ago, and that system is patterned after a national system devised more than two centuries ago. However, one of the glories of the national governmental and political systems has been their tendency to permit or even encourage political change that has accommodated changing national and international circumstances. Regrettably, New Mexico government and politics have been less responsive. The fundamental and traditional style of culturally based, locally oriented, defensive, and incremental politics continues through the decades. With infrequent exceptions, leadership has failed to emerge in order to provide a focus for government and the citizenry. Most political officials exhibit a lack of vision or concern for the entire public, concentrating instead on serving narrow interests over a short run of time. Attempts at leadership are typically opposed by status-quo interests.

It is difficult to believe that it is for lack of industriousness, concern, or ability that New Mexicans have an archaic and inadequate governmental system, for from the beginning, New Mexicans have been an industrious and intelligent people who have accomplished much in spite of minimal resources and who have persevered through rather difficult circumstances. Yet there seems to be a kind of suspicion or distrust among the public with regard to the role of government or politics as an active problem solver for our state. In truth, even when public figures have tried to exert some leadership, they typically have been soundly and, sometimes, unfairly criticized, and then once again forced to resume a low profile. New Mexicans have been given several opportunities to reform institutions and even to overhaul the constitution, and these attempts also have been rebuffed by the voting public.

Our hypothesis contends that this poor performance by government is the result of the fact that its primary, if covert or implicit, function has been to accommodate the tensions and potential conflicts inherent in a fragmented political culture. Ethnic-racial, religious, and regional differences have been so mutually reinforcing and so distinctive that they have posed a major threat to the stability of the system. The system and the people have opted to direct their public conflict-resolving mechanisms—politics and government—toward the employ-ment of their resources in dampening and resolving this basic conflict. One must admit that in keeping social order in a

culturally diverse society, New Mexico politics and government have performed admirably.

It is unfortunate, however, that our governmental and
political systems cannot get beyond this point, for New Mexico
is experiencing a period of rapid and increasing change, such as
the one immediately following World War II. The composition
of the population is changing, as well as its economic base. A
wide variety of new needs and demands are being levied upon
our governmental system. Yet the response, by and large, has
been half hearted and inadequate. As the pace of technological
change quickens and New Mexico is increasingly drawn into
national and international matters, the creativity and ingenu-
ity of the people somehow must meet the challenge of an
antiquated constitution and an archaic political system.

Writing in the early 1950s, Thomas Donnelly stated that
even four decades ago there was a great need for improved
health and welfare, social, and educational services in New
Mexico. Perhaps as an aside, and perhaps subconsciously very
tellingly, he stated that it was "only through improved economic conditions" that the welfare of the state could be
enhanced. But where will these improved economic stimuli
come from? What role, if any, will there be for government in
encouraging and supporting such improvement in economic
conditions? Perhaps the stimuli must come from the public
itself. Regrettably, the situation may first have to become so
bad that the public will be forced to override its accom-
modationist, conservative, and segmented self-interest, and
demand governmental reform. There may have to be major
alterations in the state's political culture—changes that are
veritably trauma induced—before the state's politics and government will be transformed.

Forty years ago, Thomas Donnelly thought that "improvement in [social service] matters is dependent upon an aroused

public opinion which will demand adequate financial support"
(155). Perhaps after five decades of relative unresponsiveness
and sometimes outright irresponsibility, New Mexico's government and politics will assume its appropriate, twentieth-
century responsibilities before the twenty-first century arrives.
Twenty-five years ago, Jack Holmes wrote that "groups and
areas . . . have clung steadfastly to . . . habits of political
behavior. Their political style . . . has so far changed but little
in fifty years, although more critical changes of behavior may
be in the offing" (268).

In the last decade of the twentieth century, we must
observe: not yet.

BIBLIOGRAPHY

Unfortunately, the readily available published literature on New
Mexico politics and government is as undeveloped as its subject.
Although politics has always been extremely important to the state
and very salient to its citizens, this has not been reflected in writings
on the subject. Especially lacking are comprehensive overviews.
There have been only three such book-length, comprehensive
monographs produced in the last 50 years. Thomas Donnelly, finding
that "no work was available on the government of New Mexico,"
produced the first edition of *The Government of New Mexico*, published
by the University of New Mexico Press in 1947. A revised and updated
revision of the volume was published in 1953. Another three decades
passed before the next comprehensive work on the state's government
was produced. *New Mexico Government*, ed. by F. Chris Garcia and
Paul L. Hain, was published in its first edition by the University of
New Mexico Press in 1976. It featured twelve chapters, each written
by experts in their respective fields. A revised edition by the two
University of New Mexico professors became available in 1981, and
a third edition is now nearing completion.

The most current, comprehensive—if less detailed—volume was

published in 1990 by the University Press of America. *New Mexico Government and Politics* was authored by Maurilio E. Vigil, Michael Olsen, and Roy Lujan. It is an outgrowth of a background document prepared for a town-hall meeting of New Mexico First. Although it is a less in-depth treatment of the subject, it is a lively and concise exposition.

A fourth volume, very detailed although not comprehensive in its coverage, is the excellent scholarly volume by Jack E. Holmes, *Politics in New Mexico* (Albuquerque: University of New Mexico Press, 1967). This work focuses on the political parties in the state, particularly as they are manifested in voting, in the legislature, and in the governorship. In addition to including a great deal of quantitative and qualitative analysis of party activities, this work is valuable for its insightful treatment of Hispanics in New Mexico politics and of the distinctive political cultures of the state.

Another overview, albeit one of essay length, is the article by Professors Harry P. Stumpf and T. Phillip Wolf, "New Mexico: The Political State," in *Politics in the American West*, ed. Frank H. Jonas (Salt Lake City: University of Utah Press, 1969), 258–95. With an optimistic and hopeful overtone, the authors capture many of the changing circumstances of the period from post-World War II to the late 1960s.

Dorothy I. Cline, professor emeritus of the University of New Mexico, is one of the most astute and prolific writers on New Mexico government and politics. Many of her works focus on the New Mexico Constitution. See, for example, her small book on *New Mexico's 1910 Constitution* (Santa Fe: Lightning Tree Press, 1985). Also focusing on the New Mexico Constitution, more particularly on its piecemeal amendment, is a report by Richard H. Folmar, of the New Mexico Legislative Council Service, entitled "Piecemeal Amendment of the New Mexico Constitution, 1911 to 1973," a very comprehensive review of the state constitution. Suggestions for revision are found in the "Report of the Constitutional Revision Commission, State of New Mexico, 1967." More narrowly focused on reorganization of the executive branch is "Responsive Government, 1978, the Governor's Fiscal Report on the Reorganization of the Executive Branch of New

Mexico State Government, 1977." The background to this proposal and the politics which led to the enactment of some of its recommendations are covered in "Reorganization of the Executive Branch of State Government: New Mexico, 1975–78" by Dorothy I. Cline, 1978. It was reprinted as Number 85 in the series produced by UNM's Division of Government Research. In her report, Professor Cline refers to Folmar's comprehensive government report as a "modern version of the Little Hoover report," which was produced as the "Report, New Mexico State Reorganization Committee, 1952." This earlier report is also a thorough examination of the New Mexico Constitution and offers similar recommendations for its revision and reform, as did, later, the reports of the Constitutional Revision Commission and the ensuing Constitutional Convention of 1969.

Several articles and reports have been written about each of the major institutions and processes of New Mexico government as they have operated over the past half-century. Focusing on ethnicity and urbanization, and their effects on elections and legislative politics, is Robert D. Wrinkle, "New Mexico," in *Rocky Mountain Urban Politics*, ed. JeDon A. Emenhiser (Logan: Utah State University, 1971), 112–26.

A series of articles on elections in New Mexico was begun by Dr. Frederick C. Irion, who analyzed the elections of 1956, 1958, 1960, and 1962. Published in the *Western Political Quarterly*, these studies were subsequently continued by Dr. T. Phillip Wolf from 1964 through 1972. These include the following: "The 1966 Election in New Mexico," *Western Political Quarterly* 20 (June 1967): 586–92; (2) "The 1968 Elections in New Mexico," *Western Political Quarterly* 22 (September 1969): 510–16; and (3) "The 1970 Election in New Mexico," *Western Political Quarterly* 24 (June 1971): 316–24.

Surprisingly, there are very few objective and readily obtainable studies published about major institutions of New Mexico government, such as the legislature, the courts, or the executive branch. Many of the best are found in an impressive series of more than eighty reports produced by UNM's Division of Government Research from 1946 to 1979. The most inclusive is a brief but critically perceptive view of the major institutions and processes, written in 1956, by Drs. Charles B.

Judah and Frederick C. Irion. Entitled *The 47th State: An Appraisal of Its Government*, it is Number 49 in the series. A somewhat dated summary of the New Mexico Legislature is Richard Folmar, "Legislature 1967: A New Mexico Profile," in *Legislative Politics in the Rocky Mountain West*, ed. Suzanne A. Stoiber (Boulder: Bureau of Governmental Research and Service, University of Colorado, 1957), 51–62.

Most studies of political or governmental institutions or processes are either journalistic accounts or unpublished research by scholars. Many of the latter can be found among the master's theses and doctoral dissertations completed at the University of New Mexico and housed in its Zimmerman Library.

In addition to the published works noted above, particularly the more comprehensive volumes mentioned in the beginning of the essay, the best way to be informed about New Mexico politics and government is through the daily newspapers of the state. Among those with the widest availability, that is, circulation, and the most complete coverage of state government politics are *The Albuquerque Journal, The Albuquerque Tribune, The Santa Fe New Mexican,* and *The Santa Fe Reporter.*

THREE

A LAND OF EXTREMES

THE ECONOMY OF MODERN
NEW MEXICO, 1940–1990

MICHAEL WELSH

FRENCH historians in the midtwentieth century developed a research technique known as the *"Annales* school," which emphasized study of regions over extended periods of time (the *"longue duree"* concept) and in great depth (*"histoire totale"*). The New Mexican experience contains both variables of expanded time and breadth. Yet its scholars have moved slowly to analyze the meaning of modern life since the turn of the century, preferring to focus on the state's cultural and ethnic landscape than on its economic and business contours.

This narrow reading of the state's past leaves general audiences with little understanding of the market forces of capital, labor, environmental conditions, and ethnicity that influence New Mexican economic policymakers. Much has changed since 1940 to improve the lifestyle and opportunities for the advancement of New Mexicans, whether native or newcomer. Yet conditions that have prevailed for centuries, if not for millennia, mitigate against the fulfillment of the dreams set forth in the myriad of economic development plans and strategies emanating from the state capital in Santa Fe, the federal research laboratories in Los Alamos and Albuquerque, or the centers of academic inquiry in Las Cruces and elsewhere. It is small wonder, then, that an oft-quoted remark of a nine-teenth-century territorial governor, General Lew Wallace, still rings true: "Whatever works elsewhere in the United States will not work in New Mexico."

Three variables—factors of environment, culture, and per-ception—animate the behavior and thinking of local residents and outside observers alike when calculating the financial fortunes of the state. These in turn are anchored by three sources of capital, none of them internal: tourism, federal/state/local government, and natural resource extraction. Added to these factors are the logistical hurdles awaiting the student of economic history: the massive quantities of data, reports, and studies about New Mexico's potential and missed opportuni-ties, and the speculative nature of economic modeling and theory. Finally, one confronts the ideological persuasions of the supporters and critics of the American capitalist order: those who see urban industrial society as the culmination of centu-ries of progress, and plead for its maintenance; and those who decry the excesses and abuses of an economy that generates low-wage employment, degradation of the natural landscape, and corruption in high places of finance and government.

These obstacles, however, are not insurmountable in the study of economic history. Journalists, historians, and social scientists write at length about a variety of regional and na-tional features of economic life, much of which is applicable to the New Mexican experience. Something else must stand in the way of a fuller explication of the ways in which the New Mexico economy parallels and deviates from national and regional standards. Perusal of textbooks on the state, from the early twentieth century to the present, reveals at best a modest assessment of the role of money and power in the building of New Mexico. This is not atypical of the state's peers in the

West, although a cursory review of such texts shows that the more prosperous the state, the more willingly a textbook author addresses economic conditions and controversies.

What separates the writing of New Mexico history from that of its neighbors and of the nation is the role played by ethnicity and culture in the saga of New Mexican life. In marketplace terminology, the "consumer has spoken," and the preference is clear: readers at home and elsewhere are drawn to the "otherworldliness" and "timelessness" that artful chroniclers of the New Mexican experience have conveyed. New Mexico has been presented as a place of escape from the trauma of modernization; a place where natural tensions of politics, economics, and social and cultural distinctions either do not intrude or have been reconciled and tempered. Whether such is true or not, consumers weary of the modern and the innovative flock to New Mexico's cultural fairs and sites, hoping that a state which in 1991 ranked forty-sixth in the nation in per-capita income might provide pleasures and diversions they cannot find at home.

This duality appears in a thousand ways, and its coercive powers have constricted the dialogue about how and why New Mexicans live the way they do. Consider, for example, the following occurrence in the late 1980s, during the administration of Republican Governor Garrey Carruthers, noted for his "pro-business" attitudes and conservative political beliefs. In the *New Mexico Magazine*, a publication of the state's tourism and economic-development office, advertisements for an expensive Santa Fe hotel showed the deep blue sky, tawny adobe colors, and multihued population of the "City Different," with a caption reading: "It's Not New; It's Not Mexico." Then the same administration's Department of Motor Vehicles changed the state's license plates to read, "New Mexico, U.S.A.," alongside the "Land of Enchantment" logo, in order to reassure drivers about the state's schizophrenic North American-Latin American image.

This effort to balance two worlds of understanding demonstrates the power of the marketplace to shape the consumption of New Mexican cultural and ethnic tradition, whether this includes the state's ancient foodways and ceremonial life or contemporary and tawdry manifestations such as the sale of rubber tomahawks in Old Town Albuquerque or howling coyotes on the Santa Fe Plaza. Sifting through these challenges of perception, methodology, and ideology thus presents the student of modern New Mexico with an excellent opportunity to tell a story that is desperately needed, especially in light of changes in the international economy that bode ill for any state that ignores their impact.

To that end, the student can follow two approaches that expand an understanding of the economy of modern New Mexico; one thematic and one statistical. By linking ideas and data, one can energize the writing not only of recent history, but also examine the continuity of events and issues that have brought the New Mexican economy to the close of the twentieth century. This author calls these themes the "Three-E's" of contemporary New Mexico: the environmental, electoral, and ethnic economies. Each has its strengths and weaknesses as explainers and predictors of state financial realities, and each also offers contrasts and comparisons that answer the more vexing questions about New Mexico's standing vis-à-vis its neighbors and the country as a whole.

A common lament about Americans by European scholars is that the United States has no sense of the power of the past to shape the present and future. As a young society, Americans still cling to the assumption that the future must be better than the past, even as nostalgia sweeps the country in search of windows revealing a simpler life. New Mexico's economic conditions at the close of the twentieth century stemmed from its heritage of geographic isolation from the centers of foreign power (Madrid, Mexico City, and Washington, D.C.) that ruled the Southwest for the past five centuries; its environmental extremes of aridity, short growing seasons, and the fragility of plant and animal life; and its highly diffuse ethnic populations. Ironically, these obstructions also have appealed to many escapees from the hectic pace of modernity, whether from sixteenth-century Europe or twentieth-century California, Texas, and New York.

Two economic reports from long ago offer a perspective for a study of the last five decades of New Mexican economic affairs. The first Spanish explorer of the Southwest, the twenty-six-year-old Francisco Vásquez de Coronado, encountered only grief and pain in his quest for the "golden dream" of Quivira. In his report to the Spanish royal officials in 1542, a chastened Coronado spoke simply and directly to the burdens awaiting any future conqueror. He noted that the environment was harsh (the "Llano Estacado" of the Great Plains was but the most severe among many challenges facing Coronado); the native cultures would resist domination; and the cost of recreating the Spanish world in the Southwest would be prohibitive, requiring massive and permanent subsidies from a royal treasury that would find no more golden lands like Mexico or Peru.

Nearly three centuries later, at the close of the Spanish era in New Mexico, don Pedro Pino, a prosperous landowner, traveled to Madrid to deliver to the Spanish Cortes (or legislature) the complaints of its citizens. Since the Spanish government by 1810 had been unable to change dramatically the human or natural conditions of the Southwest, Pino's report (which went unheeded) pleaded for more royal funds for economic development and social services.

American travelers and officials to New Mexico in the

nineteenth century, not having read the works of Coronado or Pino, eerily echoed their concerns and added their own cultural biases to their explanations for economic realities. Josiah Gregg, author of *Commerce of the Prairies*, his reminiscences of travels down the Santa Fe Trail in the 1830s and 1840s, had few kind words for the perspicacity of the New Mexican merchant, even as he grudgingly acknowledged the shrewdness and imagination of the region's business elite. Army officers stationed in New Mexico after 1846 commented at length on the lack of amenities, as did visitors as diverse as Susan Shelby Magoffin, in 1846, or Mabel Dodge (later Luhan), in 1917.

By the early twentieth century the arrival of American technology, primarily the railroad, and investment capital had transformed the means of doing business in the territory. Many texts speak to the outrages of the "Santa Fe Ring," the collection of business and political leaders, both Anglo and Hispanic, who mimicked the Gilded Age phenomenon of ambitious men using government to advance their private economic concerns. The wealthiest man in New Mexico was purportedly the lawyer Thomas Benton Catron, who parlayed his position as U.S. Attorney in the land-grant cases of the 1860s and 1870s to amass a fortune in land and natural resources. However the economic tapestry was woven, New Mexicans interested in participating in the national business arena had to adapt to the free-market impulses that used the territory's resources and labor to transfer wealth to the East Coast or to Europe.

The gift of statehood bestowed upon New Mexico in 1912 did not usher in the promised land of prosperity that promoters like Governor Miguel Antonio Otero (1897–1906) had suggested when he led the territory toward a progressive model of good government and efficient resource development. The earliest data on New Mexico's financial standing (the 1920 census) found per-capita income to be forty-seventh out of

forty-eight states. Only 325,000 people inhabited New Mexico's
121,000 square miles (a ratio just barely greater than Frederick
Jackson Turner's 1893 indicator of 2 people per square mile that
proclaimed the "closing of the frontier"). At 18,000 people,
Albuquerque ranked as the state's only "large" city, and the
public school system had less than two dozen high schools.

From such thresholds, the New Mexican economy had
very little distance to fall when the Wall Street stock market
crashed in October 1929. New Mexico textbooks present the
bravado of state political leaders in the early 1930s in declaring
that the state entered the depression in better shape than the
more urban sectors of America and thus needed fewer social-
welfare programs and charitable activities. In 1930, however,
New Mexico remained at the bottom of per-capita-income
statistics, and ranked first in public illiteracy, child and infant
mortality, and other indicators of social stress.

The arrival of the federal social-welfare programs of Franklin
D. Roosevelt and his "New Deal" came none too soon for New
Mexicans of every ethnic and economic persuasion. In the
1920s, when more "free-market" conditions prevailed, 60 percent of the state's 120 banks closed their doors, and many
investors lost their life savings. The state's 1932 per-capita
income of 209 dollars stood at 52 percent of the national
average, and would not achieve predepression totals for the
remainder of the decade. One-third of all schoolchildren did not
attend class in 1933, and also that year professors at the University
of New Mexico received only two months' salary. Total state
personal income fell almost 54 percent, and state leaders
encountered much opposition to their conservative dislike of
federal spending programs for economic recovery and relief.

By reaching out to Washington for support in its time of
need, New Mexico merely reestablished ties forged in the
territorial era (1846–1912), when Congress appropriated much

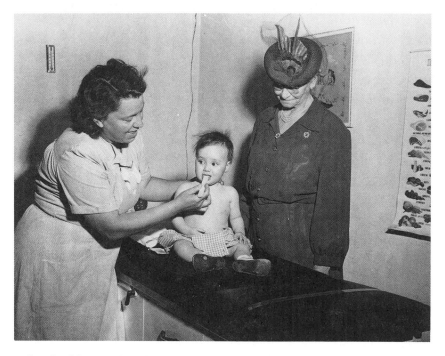

Infant health care. Photo by E. Dale Britton. (Courtesy Center for Southwest Research, General Library, University of New Mexico, neg. no. 000-294-0030.)

of the operating capital for public works and services. From the earliest days of the Roosevelt administration, New Mexicans saw what the government called "transfer payments" pour in on a massive scale. In 1929, only 1.8 percent of all New Mexican income could be classified as "disbursements for which no services are required." By 1936 this amount had leaped nearly fourfold (to 6 percent), helping the state's total income almost approximate 1929 levels. Ten years later (1946), transfer payments had stabilized at 7 percent of total income, a figure that continued throughout the remainder of the twentieth century.

Despite the "safety net" that New Deal social programs offered New Mexicans, economic life had not improved substantially for the state by the close of the 1930s. Conservative commentators nationwide pointed to the cycle of dependency that federal payments generated, ignoring the fact that subsistence wages and temporary employment were too modest to spark the consumer revival that would allow the marketplace to resume control of the nation's economic life. New Mexico relied upon its progressive-to-liberal coterie of state and congressional leaders—especially Bronson Cutting, Dennis Chavez, Clinton Anderson, Carl Hatch, and Clyde Tingley—to secure federal grants for every conceivable program, from construction of Conchas Dam near Tucumcari (at 15 million dollars in 1935, a sum greater than the total New Mexican state budget) to Works Progress Administration employment for low-skilled laborers and the Santa Fe and Taos art colonies alike. By 1936 New Mexico ranked last in the nation in state matching funds for New Deal programs, having paid to Washington a mere three-quarters of 1 percent of the total cost of grants disbursed statewide. Unemployment in 1939 still stood in excess of 1929 averages, 30 percent of families earned less than one hundred dollars annually (the total state per-capita income was four hundred dollars), and the future anchors of the postwar economy, tourism and government, employed but 5 and 4 percent of the work force, respectively.

The most salient feature of American economic life since 1940 has been the dramatic escalation in the standard of living. Population increases nationwide have been more modest, from 140 million to 260 million, or a fifty-year rise of less than 55 percent. Yet national per-capita income has grown from 595 dollars (1940) to 18,691 dollars (1990), or over thirty-one times. Even if one adjusts for inflation, the inescapable fact is that Americans earn much more than they did on the eve of World War II. New Mexico took a similar journey, moving since 1940 in population from 360,000 to 1.6 million (a factor of five), and in per-capita income from 375 dollars to 14,256 dollars (an increase of thirty-nine times). In that vein, one could argue that New Mexico has outperformed the nation as a whole in both population and income growth and that the state should be a case study for both economists and historians interested in the ability of the American economy to deliver on its promises.

Yet closer perusal of the data and the state's environmental, political, and ethnic variables provides a clearer perspective of the concerns and complaints that emanate from every corner of New Mexico about its economic health. In justifying his tax cuts in 1962, President John F. Kennedy often quoted the cliché, "A rising tide lifts all boats." Unmentioned was the persistence of the comparative status quo, with more prosperous states continuing their dominance of the national economic scene, while pockets of poverty and depression remained in the backwaters and eddys of the national economy. These factors also touched the New Mexican economy in the second half of the twentieth century, and the concerns at the century's close about constrained public spending, environmental depletion, and fiscal instability called for more sober and thoughtful assessments of the forces that shaped New Mexico's economic life.

The ancient Greeks, who knew something about the meaning of war, believed that, whatever its benefits, war had a destabilizing effect upon society that would take years to understand, let alone correct. Starting in 1940, every indicator one chooses about New Mexico's economic life showed upward trajectories. Searching for low-cost, open-space territory, military strategists and White House planners turned to the Southwest and Pacific Coast states to build military installations, defense plants, and transportation networks. From 1941 to 1945, the War Department located twenty-one separate military bases, training centers, prisoner-of-war, and Japanese internment camps within New Mexico. The multimillion-dollar federal facilities at Los Alamos, Sandia Base, and the Alamogordo

A replica of Fat Man, the atomic bomb detonated over the Trinity Site and Nagasaki, Japan, stands on display at the National Atomic Museum in Albuquerque. (Courtesy National Atomic Museum.)

Bombing Range were but the most dramatic evidence of the economic power of a war economy. The imperatives of national security, the national wage scales of the federal government, and the patriotism that washed across the landscape, in turn made federal military investment highly attractive to the state's leaders.

Statistics for the years from 1940 to 1945 reveal the scale and scope of the political economy, which reverberated throughout the state for decades to come. People flocked to the state's urban centers, like Albuquerque, doubling its population every five years. More dramatic was the increase in personal income, which grew 250 percent, and stood four times greater than 1932 levels. New Mexicans joined the national diaspora from the farm to the city during these years, as enlistments, urban employment, or declining birthrates drove downward the state's rural population. By 1950 farmwork, the staple of New Mexican income prior to 1940, had dropped to 17.3 percent, even as personal income for the decade leaped fourfold.

Victory over the Japanese in the Pacific theater, and over Germany in Europe, posed a challenging question for New Mexican leaders. The forces that had energized the state, and the tide that indeed "lifted all boats," were fading. The historic demobilization of the armed services left New Mexico in 1945-46 without an equivalent source of income, and the growing mood of conservatism nationwide did not augur well for social-welfare programs. Inflation, cuts in military spending, and the awkward return to consumer production drove the national and state per-capita incomes downward in 1946, only to be revived the following year, when the "Cold War" between the United States and the Soviet Union reached crisis proportions. Military bases remained open, the nuclear research facility at Los Alamos received a new lease on life, and the heralded "baby boom" of increased birthrates merged with the postwar migration later called the "Sunbelt boom" to continue the stream of people and dollars to New Mexico and the West.

The source of income that persisted for New Mexicans before and after World War II was use of the natural environment. From the earliest Native societies and, later, the Spaniards to the 1930s, stockraising and farming had underpinned whatever prosperity the region had known. But what the nation needed during and after the Second World War was energy. Oil and gas revenues, timber, coal and copper mining, and uranium mining all contributed to the expansion of New Mexican wages and salaries in the postwar era. Enough money flowed to state coffers in taxes and royalties to subsidize such necessities as public schools, the transportation infrastructure, and social-welfare services. Assessment of the growth of such counties as San Juan, Lea, Valencia (Cibola, after 1981), and Grant showed the reliance upon resource extraction and the good fortune that rippled throughout those counties' economic networks.

Two factors appeared in the latter decades of the twentieth century, however, to alter the resource equation of New Mexico. From extraction to processing, to distribution of the state's oil, gas, coal, uranium, and copper, all sectors of the resource economy suffered from the challenge of environmental activism and the decline of national and international markets. Wages and tax revenues slipped or vanished in the face of a "bust" cycle not unfamiliar to regional historians and economists, but which affected many aspects of New Mexican life far from the camps, mines, oilfields, and uranium pits. Tuition at state institutions of higher learning, like the University of New Mexico, rose 105 percent from 1985 to 1990, and demands for social-welfare programs escalated as workers lost their jobs, their health-care and insurance benefits, and their homes.

By most standards of measurement, the decade of the 1950s was the best that New Mexico had ever seen. Federal wages grew by a factor of ten, total personal income grew by 250 percent, and transfer payments became, as they had been prior to 1933, a minor feature of the total state budget (only 97 million dollars of the state's 1.7-billion-dollar income by 1959). The resource economy played its part in this celebration of prosperity, leaping 201.9 percent during the decade, spurred by wage increases in natural-gas production of 696.6 percent. The uranium economy drove the population of Grants from nothing in 1940 to 2,251 ten years later, and to 10,274 by 1960. Resource income in Valencia County, where Grants was located, leaped seven times in the decade, allowing for a doubling of county per-capita income despite only a 25-percent increase in government spending.

Political leaders in New Mexico like Clinton Anderson, Dennis Chavez, and others could look with pride on the accomplishments of their state as the decade of the 1950s drew to a close. Whereas the nation as a whole had witnessed three economic recessions, the presence of a vast military-industrial complex prompted Ralph Edgel, director of the UNM Bureau of Business Research, to declare in 1961 that "during the postwar period New Mexico's economy has been singularly insulated from the effects" of the national slowdowns. By 1959 the federal government, with 218 separate offices representing 33 agencies, employed 17.3 percent of all New Mexicans. Testimony to the value of federal wage scales was the 21.3 percent that federal employees earned of all New Mexican wages that year (some 20 percent higher than nonfederal employment).

As with all success stories, there was evidence of trouble in other sectors of the New Mexican economy in the 1950s. For the first time in 1950, half of all New Mexicans lived in cities, a percentage that the United States had reached thirty years earlier. Four thousand farms went out of production in the decade, and only nine of New Mexico's thirty-two counties benefited from the job growth and population increases. In the sixteen declining counties, federal spending was modest to nonexistent, and welfare and social security payments grew significantly as a result: 240 percent and 2,600 percent, respectively. State expenditures for everything from welfare to schools to roads grew 219.4 percent, while tax revenues increased only 154.3 percent, outstripping the state's increase in income (135.9 percent) for the decade.

By 1960, then, the contours of the state's postwar economy had come into focus. There would be great prosperity for those communities and individuals who understood the national and international economy, with its emphasis on information, investment, and technology. Those counties blessed with natural resources demanded by an advanced economy also shared in the good fortune. Yet these factors would touch half the state

An air traffic controller at Albuquerque's Sunport directs flight patterns over central New Mexico. (Courtesy Center for Southwest Research, General Library, University of New Mexico, neg. no. 000-299-1453.)

only marginally, and several counties (Taos, Sandoval, Mora, Rio Arriba, and San Miguel, especially) would see continued economic stagnation. Ironically, this would eventually become the pattern for the nation as a whole, when the boom of the 1980s would center on the East and West coasts, fueled by growth itself, military spending, and the lure of urban amenities.

The decade of the 1960s has been studied more for its social and political upheavals than for its economic trends nationally. Thus, it is small wonder that no data appear in New Mexico textbooks to show the decade's decline in consumer spending, federal investment, and population growth. "Hippie" communes near Taos get more attention than the fact that the state's population increased a mere 6.8 percent (a decline of 75 percent from the 1950s) or that the sixties were the first decade in a century when New Mexican growth could not be measured at least in double digits. Other numbers about poverty stand in stark contrast to the *"Happy Days"* atmosphere of the 1950s. By 1970 the state's poverty rate overall was 22.8 percent, one-quarter of all New Mexico counties had poverty rates of 32 percent or higher (Mora's rate was 57 percent), half of the state's communities of one thousand or more had lost population, 47.7 percent of all female-headed families lived in poverty, and the state ranked last in the interior West in per-capita income.

Several factors contributed to this quiescence in New Mexico's postwar economic boom. The federal government turned its attention from Cold War research to the ground war in Vietnam, redirecting military spending away from weapons research at Los Alamos and Sandia Labs and toward manpower training and support. In social-welfare spending, the "War on Poverty" and Lyndon Johnson's "Great Society" did bring more dollars to the state, but the primary purpose of these activities was tamping down urban crises, not building impoverished rural or small-town areas like the New Deal programs. Resource production fell accordingly, with oil and gas employment down 30 percent at decade's end; and uranium mining saw the closures of nuclear weapons plants curtail activities around Grants and in the San Juan Basin. When the U.S. Air Force in 1967 closed Roswell's largest employer, Walker Air Force Base, the warning of Ralph Edgel in 1961 that the state had become too dependent upon military money indeed seemed prophetic.

New Mexico's economic roller-coaster ride returned to its upward spiral, however, in the midst of the 1970s energy crisis and the conclusion of the war in Vietnam. A new generation of political leaders took control of the state's congressional delegation, committed to restoring the flow of federal capital and resource revenue to state coffers. The retirement of Clinton P. Anderson elevated the former Democrat and Albuquerque native, Republican Pete V. Domenici, to the U.S. Senate. By 1981 he had risen to the chairmanship of the Budget Committee, where all decisions on federal spending originated before a vote of the full Senate. Harrison Schmitt, a former astronaut and graduate geologist, also occupied a seat in the U.S. Senate for one term after 1976, and he pushed for additional spending on weapons and space programs for White Sands Missile Range, Kirtland, Holloman, and Cannon air force bases, and for work at the nuclear laboratories at Los Alamos and Sandia.

This dedicated effort by New Mexico's leaders resulted from two phenomena: the downsizing of the military's manpower after Vietnam, and the escalation of high-technology research on such programs as the space shuttle, laser weaponry, and nuclear energy sources. Federal spending in New Mexico doubled during the decade, growing twice as fast as the national average. All sectors of the state's economy performed in similar fashion, with the percentage of overall employment slightly more than double the U.S. average. Oil and gas production surged as a result of the international energy crises of 1973 and 1979, which escalated the price per barrel of crude oil from three dollars in 1970 to thirty-four dollars in 1981. Manufacturers were also lured to the Land of Enchantment, bringing growth of 60 percent to that sector (an increase twelve times the national average for the decade). Many of these jobs, however, were low-wage, service, and assembly positions, developed in conjunction with changing international conditions that saw the rise of low-cost production overseas or in "maquiladora" plants farther south in Mexico.

All of this growth affected state and local government, as it had in the 1950s. Santa Fe lawmakers expanded the public work force by 57 percent, and municipalities and counties added 49 percent more workers to their payrolls. In both cases, New Mexico outpaced the national increase in public employees. The state's population had increased from 1 million to 1.4 million, or a percentage of one-third. Thus, the 1950s syndrome of public services growing faster than the rate of population had returned, and the 1980s promised more of the same. Added to this were concerns about the erosion of New Mexico's "quality of life," much like the national debate over the dark side of economic growth in the postwar era. The Washington, D.C.-based Resources for the Future published in 1981 a study entitled *The Southwest under Stress*, which argued that prosperity had begun to haunt New Mexico and its neighbors, and that growth needed restraint.

The decade of the 1980s may explain why historians are so cautious about predicting the future. Where most economists and public officials proclaimed a bright future for New Mexico as the decade dawned, a historian might have noticed the cycles of boom and bust that had occurred at least since the 1930s. Warnings might have followed that the 1980s could see times more like the 1960s, with the leveling of federal spending, the volatility of energy prices, and the shift of military emphasis from advanced technology to ground forces (as in 1991's "Operation Desert Storm"). Then, of course, no historian could have envisioned the sudden collapse of the Soviet Union, taking with it the rationale for the massive military and space research of the preceding five decades. These features, nonetheless, combined in the 1980s to challenge the New Mexican economy yet again and leave economists and politicians in the 1990s guessing once more about the state's fortunes.

New Mexico's chances at economic sufficiency reached their peak in 1981, when per-capita income, buoyed by energy production, reached thirty-eighth place nationally. Yet the ripple effect from the 1979 nuclear plant accident at Three Mile

Island, Pennsylvania, dampened enthusiasm for nuclear energy and the production of uranium. New Mexico's possession of 55 percent of the nation's uranium resources suddenly became a liability rather than an asset, and the population of Grants declined as fast as rural farm and ranch counties had in the 1950s. The deregulation of oil by the Reagan administration in the early 1980s also did not trigger a sustained production boom.

The free-fall of oil prices in 1986 crushed the state's oil industry, the decline of which at 49.2 percent was nearly double the national average (itself a substantial 28 percent below 1980 levels). Only state and local government could step in to staunch the flow of unemployment, adding nearly 28 percent more workers to their payrolls, even as oil royalties and severance taxes shrunk precipitously (oil and gas taxes and royalties had paid 55 percent of the state's costs of public education in 1980; a figure that fell to less than 15 percent by 1990). This also marked a major advance over New Mexico's erstwhile patron, the federal government, whose spending in the state would increase only four-tenths of 1 percent in the decade (a growth rate only one-sixth the national average).

By 1990 the outlook for the New Mexico economy was decidedly mixed, a reflection also of national trends. The UNM Bureau of Business and Economic Research (BBER), in its December 1991 report, noted the uncertainty of conditions statewide and in the Albuquerque metropolitan area. In the late 1980s, the state could claim that it had avoided much of the trauma afflicting the East and West coasts with the end of the double-digit-percentage increases in defense spending. A booming market for second homes in Santa Fe and Taos for refugees from the high costs and social problems of American cities had created expectations for more. Santa Fe housing prices, driven by the California "equity spiral," had reached figures beyond the capacity of 95 percent of local residents to purchase, while

The clean room at Intel Corporation ensures a dust-free environment for the manufacture of silicon chips. (Courtesy Intel Corporation.)

the demand for "high-end" homes valued from 250,000 dollars to 1 million dollars continued unabated. Even the reshuffling of military personnel and bases prompted by the end of the Cold War redounded to New Mexico's benefit, as none of the state's facilities lost large numbers of jobs and in fact gained at the expense of other locales.

Statistics for 1986, however, revealed that the pride taken by New Mexican officials would yet again be tested by the historical realities of the marketplace. Government employment stood at 26.1 percent of the work force, compared to 16.7 percent nationally. In manufacturing, despite all the gains of the postwar era, only 7.1 percent of all New Mexican workers had factory jobs, compared to the national average of 19 percent. Per-capita income kept slipping throughout the decade, and by 1990 New Mexico again settled into the bottom 10 percent of states, ranking forty-sixth out of fifty. It was not surprising, then, to read in the BBER's 1991 report that despite New Mexico's good fortune to date, one in four residents had no health insurance, over one in five lived below the poverty line (the national average was one in seven), and, as Brian McDonald wrote, "New Mexico's high dependence on defense spending still presents a major risk to the state's economy in the 1990s."

What that economy had become after five decades of struggle and accomplishment would not be clear for some time. Yet glimpses of the journey appeared soon after the 1990 census. By 1991 New Mexico had retreated to 76 percent of the U.S. per-capita income, a figure that the state had last seen in 1948. Despite the state's income of 14,256 dollars per person in 1990 (an average of ten dollars per hour in wages based upon a two-thousand-hour work year), workers earned nearly five thousand dollars less per year than their peers nationwide. This explained the need for increased state and local government employment, and the acceleration of trends already established in the 1980s to bring more tourists, attract more retirees, and lure more manufacturing jobs that might otherwise move offshore or south of the border.

In 1990, the BBER released data on the ninety-three employers in New Mexico that hired more than five hundred workers. Although economists often pay lip service to the virtues of "small business," most indicators of a state's economic health look to the large job producers, as these provide the most stable benefits and career ladders for their employees. A scan of the organizations listed offered a suggestion of the future economy that scholars would analyze decades hence. Fifty years after the start of World War II, New Mexico's largest employer had become the University of New Mexico, at twelve-thousand full- and part-time workers a far cry from the campus of 1945 that had but six hundred students. Indeed, the ten largest employers were all state, federal, or local government entities. The largest private employer was Wal-Mart department stores, at thirty-eight hundred workers a mere shadow of UNM, and the largest private corporation headquartered in New Mexico was the Clovis-based Allsup's convenience stores, which employed twenty-four hundred (one-fifth of UNM's total). In all, fourteen of New Mexico's top ninety-three employers were public school systems; eleven more were hospitals or health-care organizations; four were colleges, universities, or trade schools; and twenty were federal, state, and local government service agencies, for a total of forty-nine employers (53 percent) whose income derived from tax revenue or health insurance.

Two features of the postwar New Mexican economy, then, remained constant as the twentieth century closed. The state's multicultural population and heritage served as a lure for tourists seeking the unusual and different in American environment and ethnicity, especially with the reawakening of interest in historical traditions and cultural diversity. The reliance upon government at all levels to undergird the daily life of New Mexicans also held sway, as natural-resource development or advanced technology research and production shifted with the economic tides of the international marketplace. Both sectors of strength, however, had their unintended consequences. The Native and Hispanic peoples of the state, particularly those artisans and crafts makers of the northern villages and towns, debated in the 1990s the wisdom of transmitting their culture and heritage to strangers for cash. Publications as diverse as the *Santa Fe Reporter* and the state's own *New Mexico Magazine* noted the resistance of Hispanic and Indian communities to the intrusiveness of tourism, even as they carried advertisements for the massive "Indian Market" in Santa Fe every August, where a state-conducted survey claimed that the one thousand artisans at the eight hundred booths generated 130 million dollars in trade over a two-day weekend. When, in 1992, the state tourism department produced national advertising marketing the Good Friday journey of New Mexican Catholics to the sacred shrine of the Santuario de Chimayo, the letters-to-the-editor columns of state newspapers filled with comments about the burden of tourism and the pain it inflicted upon a state where visitors generated 2.4 billion dollars annually and thirty-four thousand jobs.

In like manner, the continued dependence of New Mexico upon tax revenues for provision of employment as well as social services boded ill for a healthy and varied private economy. Throughout the 1980s the state had ranked between fourth and first in federal spending per capita, even as the personal-income rankings fell from thirty-eighth to forty-seventh. By 1991 New Mexicans stood ninth nationally in total amounts of state and local taxes paid, even though over 40 percent of families earned less than 15,000 dollars (a statistic more telling than the personal levels of 14,256 dollars).

Given New Mexico's emphasis on folk culture and tradition, a folk saying about the contemporary economy might explain the dichotomy between the state's attractiveness and modest economic achievements. The story went that the state chamber of commerce told visitors that once they came to New Mexico, they would fall in love with its environment and cultures, and never leave. More sober judgments by residents held that the *dicho* should read just the opposite: once one comes to New Mexico, one gets so poor one cannot leave. Whether one is cynical or satisfied, the lessons of the post-1940 economy are clear. New Mexico offers a mirror upon the past and future of the United States. Building the nation took much energy, used much of the natural landscape, and required laborers from around the world to deny their heritages as they assimilated into the mainstream of society. Now that the nation has matured, reflects back upon its life of abundance, and faces a future of scarcity, Americans (and visitors from around the world) seek in New Mexico a tranquility and sense of place that is missing elsewhere. Unfortunately, scholars of the New Mexican experience must address these inconsistencies more honestly, including the search for prosperity and wealth, or else another generation of natives and newcomers will never know why the dream of a good life that people bring to New Mexico fails to resonate at home.

BIBLIOGRAPHY

As with much historical writing about twentieth-century New Mexico, no single volume furnishes a full account of the modernization of the state's economy since the outbreak of World War II. The standard textbooks are often anecdotal, as in Marc Simmons, *New Mexico: A Bicentennial History* (New York: W. W. Norton, 1977), or Erna Fergusson, *New Mexico: A Pageant of Three Peoples* (Albuquerque: University of New Mexico Press, 1951, 1962). Despite its questionable assumptions about New Mexican culture and ethnicity, the best effort to integrate economic statistics into the story of the state is Warren Beck, *New Mexico: A History of Four Centuries* (Norman: University of Oklahoma, 1962). Calvin Roberts and Susan Roberts, *New Mexico* (Albuquerque: University of New Mexico Press, 1988), includes statistical analysis in its standard themes of railroads, mining, livestock, and the nuclear economy.

If thoroughgoing treatments of the state's economic development are absent from textbooks or monographs, the more general literature of the American West written by historians or journalists also gives little attention to the New Mexico economy. Gerald D. Nash, *The American West in the Twentieth Century: A Short History of an Urban Oasis* (Albuquerque: University of New Mexico Press, 1977), and Michael P. Malone and Richard W. Etulain, *The American West: A Twentieth-Century History* (Lincoln: University of Nebraska

Press, 1989), refer to the state's economic life only briefly, focusing on the broader outlines of the region's existence since 1900. Discussion of New Mexico's economic history also appears in the dated text of W. Eugene Hollon, *The Southwest: Old and New* (Lincoln: University of Nebraska Press, 1961).

Neil Morgan, *Westward Tilt: The American West Today* (New York: Random House, 1963), followed in the footsteps of Morris Garnsey, *America's New Frontier: The Rocky Mountain West* (New York: Harper and Brothers, 1947), after World War II as journalists commenting upon contemporary conditions in the West. The best of the more recent journalistic endeavors is Neal R. Peirce and Jerry Hagstrom, *The Book of America: Inside 50 States Today* (New York: Norton, 1983), which offers commentary on the general outlines of the late twentieth-century economy and political structure of the state and its peers. Surprisingly, the more current and more provocative texts about regionalism written by reporters in the 1980s did little with New Mexico: Joel Garreau, *The Nine Nations of North America* (New York: Avon Books, 1982); and Peter Wiley and Robert Gottlieb, *Empires in the Sun: The Rise of the New American West* (Tucson: University of Arizona Press, 1985). Both titles devote most of their attention to New Mexico's more prosperous neighbors to the east and west: Texas and California.

To develop a more holistic vision of the state's financial and economic contours, one must break down the subject matter into discrete topics and mention the manuscript sources of the public and private entities shaping New Mexican fiscal policy since 1940. One begins with the decennial reports of the U.S. Department of Labor, and the *Statistical Abstracts*, put forth by the U.S. Department of Commerce. The state of New Mexico likewise has a series of publications entitled *The New Mexico Statistical Abstract*, published annually since 1950. One could also consult the publications of the Bureau of Business and Economic Research at the University of New Mexico (the BBER), whose compilations of data first appeared in the mid-1940s. For comparison of these numbers with the western region as a whole, especially for the early postwar years, a still-valuable source is Leonard Arrington et al., *The Changing Economic Structure of the Mountain West, 1850–1950* (Logan: Utah State University Press, 1963).

The three categories of topics that provide grounding in the development of the modern New Mexico economy are environmental, governmental, and ethnic. Each has played an important role in luring investment and settlement to the state over the years, and each has been studied in varying degrees of sophistication. Fossil fuels have been surveyed in Paige W. Christiansen, *The Story of Oil in New Mexico* (Socorro: New Mexico Bureau of Mines and Mineral Resources, 1989); but no volumes address the New Mexican coal, uranium, or copper industries. In addition, the state's timber business needs attention, with only government reports from the U.S. Forest Service available. In like manner, the state's public lands and agricultural sectors merit historical treatments, especially the impact of livestock and ranching. The politics of water have been addressed in Ira Clark, *Water in New Mexico* (University of New Mexico Press, 1987); and Michael Welsh, *U.S. Army Corps of Engineers: Albuquerque District, 1935–1985* (Albuquerque: University of New Mexico Press, 1987), analyzes the technology and political economy linked to this federal agency's role in state water development. For an interpretation of the role of "economic colonialism" in the modern era, see Arthur R. Gomez, "'The Fabulous Four Corners': Neocolonialism and Sub-regional Development in the Hinterland West, 1945–1970" (Ph.D. diss., University of New Mexico, 1990), which includes discussion of Farmington and the San Juan Basin.

Even though governmental economy reached into every region and community of New Mexico, when the state ranked in the 1980s anywhere from fourth to first in per-capita federal spending, historians have been reluctant to struggle with the mass of statistical data emanating from the census or state abstracts about the ways in which tax revenues have enhanced the life of New Mexicans. A good general introduction is Clive Thomas, ed., *Politics and Public Policy in the Contemporary American West* (Albuquerque: University of New Mexico Press, 1991), along with F. Chris Garcia and Paul L. Hain, eds.,

New Mexico Government, rev ed. (Albuquerque: University of New Mexico Press, 1981).

More specific research into the political and governmental economy comes from social scientists and journalists like Tad Bartimus and Scott McCartney, *Trinity's Children: Living along America's Nuclear Highway* (New York: Harcourt Brace Jovanovich, 1991), a study of the impact of military spending up and down Interstate Highway 25 since the 1940s. Also focusing on the economic impact of federal spending in the region has been Ann Markusen et al., *The Rise of the Gunbelt: The Military Remapping of Industrial America* (New York: Oxford University Press, 1991). Necah Stewart Furman, *Sandia National Laboratories: The Postwar Decade* (Albuquerque: University of New Mexico Press, 1989), suggests the possibilities of scholarly research on such institutions now that the Cold War and its economic imperatives have ended.

The most-studied feature of New Mexican history for any era is its cultural and ethnic dimensions. Whether in coffee-table photograph books, in biographies of famous artists like Georgia O'Keeffe, or in novels and poetry, the ethnic and cultural landscape of the state needs little explanation. Yet scholars have pursued less vigorously the economic impact of such culturally driven topics as tourism; nor have they taken to heart the call of "New West" historians like Patricia Nelson Limerick, and Donald Worster, to link subjects of culture, class, and gender to the more prosaic themes explored earlier in western historiography.

Still, much has been written on the impact of the Santa Fe and Taos art colonies or more recently on the federal programs of the New Deal in the 1930s relating to cultural preservation. New Mexico could use, however, a study for the post-1940 era like Sarah J. Deutsch, *No Separate Refuge: Culture, Class, and Gender on an Anglo-Hispanic Frontier in the American Southwest, 1880–1940* (New York: Oxford University Press, 1987), with close attention to the journey of Hispanic New Mexicans north and south of their villages during and after World War II. Charles Briggs and John R. Van Ness, *Land, Water, and Culture: New Perspectives on Hispanic Land Grants* (Albuquerque:

University of New Mexico Press, 1987), offers some insight into the economic travails facing these villages upon the modernization of the state's economy and the loss of their traditional land grants. So does William deBuys, in *Enchantment and Exploitation: The Life and Hard Times of a New Mexico Mountain Range* (Albuquerque: University of New Mexico Press, 1985). In addition, the Border Institute of New Mexico State University has produced several interesting studies of the growing economy of the international boundary between New Mexico and the Republic of Mexico; and much could be done by extending northward the work of Mario T. García, *Desert Immigrants: The Mexicans of El Paso, 1880–1920* (New Haven, Conn.: Yale University Press, 1981).

More attention needs to be paid to economic features connected to New Mexican ethnic groups. For example, Indian populations have been involved in many development schemes and programs for the bulk of the twentieth century, mostly revolving around tourism or energy resources. Sylvia Rodriguez has written several articles about the linkage of tourism to the Hispanic and Indian communities of Taos, among them "The Impact of the Ski Industry on the Rio Hondo Watershed," *Annals of Tourism Research*, 14, no. 1 (1987). The Navajos have experienced several studies of their modern economic conditions, with the best one being Garrick and Roberta Glenn Bailey, *A History of the Navajos: The Reservation Years* (Santa Fe, NM: School of American Research, 1986). Also useful for a general understanding of Indians and energy policy is Marjane Ambler, *Breaking the Iron Bonds: Indian Control of Energy Development* (Lawrence: University Press of Kansas, 1990), which covers, among other topics, the oil and gas industry of the Jicarilla Apaches.

For students of urban history, a few sources of scholarship deal with contemporary New Mexican cities. Howard N. Rabinowitz, "Albuquerque: City at a Crossroads," in Richard M. Bernard and Bradley Rice, eds. *Sunbelt Cities: Politics and Growth since World War II* (Austin: University of Texas Press, 1983), is a good but brief treatment, as is Bradford Luckingham, *The Urban Southwest: A Profile History of Albuquerque, El Paso, Phoenix, Tucson* (El Paso:

Texas Western Press, 1982). Marc Simmons, *Albuquerque: A Narrative History* (Albuquerque: University of New Mexico Press, 1982), offers only two of its twelve chapters on the history of the state's largest city since 1880. Santa Fe, fabled in popular and promotional literature in the 1980s for its "style," has yet to see a thorough analysis of its economic conditions, a story that may not mesh with the conventional wisdom about the oldest capital city in the United States. Also meriting studies are the economies of the other major New Mexican communities, especially the growth of Las Cruces and the nuclear town of Alamogordo, or the WIPP-site home, Carlsbad. In addition, students could analyze such organizations as the New Mexico Municipal League, or the data generated by the Legislative Council Service and the state legislature itself.

FOUR

MAKE-BELIEVE AND GRAFFITI
ENVISIONING NEW MEXICO FAMILIES

VIRGINIA SCHARFF

I would like to begin this discussion of a half-century of change in the lives of New Mexico families with an ethnographic description, otherwise known as a personal anecdote. My anecdote is inspired by Fred Rogers, a man perhaps better known as "Mr. Rogers" of Public Television neighborhood fame. I am acquainted with Mr. Rogers because I have a six-year-old son named Sam, who has only very recently, and to my great dismay, abandoned the warmth of the Neighborhood of Make Believe for the shrill environs of Nickelodeon. During the past six years, I have been comforted that, although my husband and son and I have lived in six different houses in four different Sunbelt states, Mr. Rogers hasn't moved. Sam has spent part or all of his weekdays with eight different day-care providers, under the supervision of heaven only knows how many care-givers or teachers. My husband, Peter, has held three different jobs, and I have taught at four different colleges. We had a second child, Annie, age eighteen months right now, and the only native New Mexican in the family. But Mr. Rogers hasn't changed jobs. He hasn't even left Pittsburgh, let alone the Neighborhood of Make Believe. His livelihood and his neighborhood have been more consistent in my life than my own.

Albuquerque children are captivated by television's Mr. Rogers's Neighborhood.
Photo by Jon Hunner.

When I moved to New Mexico two and one-half years ago, to take a position in the University of New Mexico's history department, Peter agreed to quit his own professional job and be what sociologists and personnel officers call "the trailing spouse." Fifty years ago, there was neither any such designation nor any need for the term. First of all, notwithstanding the importance of the history of migration to New Mexico and the West, most people didn't relocate nearly so often or so far in the years before the Second World War. When they did, husbands virtually never "trailed" wives. Some historians of the American West have even described female migrants as "draftees in a male enterprise."

Of course, there were plenty of women who relished moving into the West in general, and what is now New Mexico in particular (whether they came from north, south, east, or west of here), but that's not the point. The point is that families generally moved because male heads of households wanted, or were compelled, to move. Whether they liked it or not, few women had the luxury of refusing to migrate when their husbands or fathers or sons announced the decision to go. In the case of New Mexico since the seventeenth century, families moved in because of Spanish, Mexican, or U.S. government colonization plans, because of the movements of armies, and, after 1880, because of the coming of the railroad. Women and children, whatever their desires, were expected to go along with men's plans.

Family historians—like Lillian Schlissel, who followed a nineteenth-century family named Malik along a migration westward through death, trauma, and separation—have shown that moving is, to say the least, hard on families. But more broadly, humanities scholars, social scientists, corporate planners, and policymakers have barely begun to assess the increasing social and psychological costs and challenges of late twentieth-century mobility. The past fifty years, to be sure, have launched more families on the move, many of them into New Mexico. By 1980, only 54 percent of all New Mexico residents had been born in the state. In that year, a majority of residents of New Mexico's urban areas—which were the fastest growing parts of the state—had been born in other states.

My family arrived in 1989, to join that emigrant majority. As I began to explain, Peter came to Albuquerque without a job, which meant living on my professor's salary, which of course ruled out buying a house. Nothing odd in this; although New Mexicans and Americans had high rates of home ownership in the 1950s and 1960s, the percentage of Americans able to buy houses has declined substantially, across the nation, since

1973. Today, few single-income families in New Mexico or in the country can afford to become homeowners. Fortunately, Peter's skills made him a good candidate to milk New Mexico's cash cow—the government-sponsored science and defense industry, established with the advent of the Manhattan Project in 1940, now emanating from Los Alamos and Sandia Laboratories, from the military bases, and from defense subcontractors serving the bases and the labs. Thus, a few months after coming to Albuquerque, we became a two-earner family, both with professional jobs. Finally we were able to scrape up the money for a down payment on a house in a middle-class neighborhood in the near Northeast Heights, west of San Mateo Boulevard and south of Indian School Road. Finally, perhaps, we have settled in New Mexico, to live in a house of our own, and to pursue the American Dream of a safe, stable, secure family life. And so, in the spirit of Mr. Rogers's hospitality, I'd like to introduce you to some other New Mexico families by inviting you into my neighborhood.

Our house is of a design very common in Albuquerque—a two-and-a-half bedroom, flat-roofed, stucco-over-concrete-block box. It was built in 1949, and at that time it was on the northeast frontier of the city. The original owner, an Anglo midwesterner now retired from the UNM English department, came over to our house one day last fall and showed us Kodak snapshots of the then-unobstructed view of the Sandia Mountains from our front porch. Another time, he arrived with a video camera and an Argentine poet who said that, decades ago, he had written some of his best poems as a guest in the house, and wanted to take a videotape of it home to Argentina to show his family.

The English professor, his wife, and their son lived in the house for twenty years, then sold it to an art-history professor, who lived in the house a few years and then re-sold it in about

1975. The new owner was a divorced mother of three, whom I will call Elizabeth (all names I will use here have been changed to preserve confidentiality). This female head of household, a New Mexico native, a Hispanic, a white-collar worker, raised her children in the house and sold it to us in 1990 for an amount slightly below both the national median home price and the median price for a house in Albuquerque.

Most people who buy homes move into their new residences when the house is empty. Ours, in a sense, came equipped with a family. Shortly after Elizabeth accepted our offer on the house, I went after work to pick up Sam at his child-care center, and ran into a staff member who said, "I heard you bought George's mother's house." It happened that Elizabeth's college-student son, George, worked in the child-care center, and he'd figured out that the people who'd bought his mother's house were the parents of Sam, a child he knew well. For his part, Sam was very excited at the prospect of moving into the room in which George had grown up.

We also learned, when we began to move in, that Mr. and Mrs. Parra, our neighbors to the south, were Elizabeth's parents. Her father, a retired railroad worker, and her homemaker mother had moved from Belen to Albuquerque when he retired and had bought their house in order to be close to their daughter and her grandchildren.

But that was only the beginning of our involvement with Elizabeth's kin. My daughter Annie was born that summer. Like most women in the United States with children under the age of six, I am (obviously) working for wages. And like most working mothers in the United States in general, and New Mexico in particular, I had no maternity leave. I went back to work three weeks after Annie was born and, amid plenty of anxiety about turning our tiny infant over to someone whom we planned, assuredly, to pay poorly, hired a student baby-sitter to come to our house and take care of Annie. As it happened, during the four months she worked for us, this young woman was also George's girlfriend.

Elizabeth's son George thus became a regular visitor to the house he'd lived in so long, splitting his time in our neighborhood between his old home, solely occupied by his girlfriend and our baby during daytime hours, and visits with his grandparents next door. In fact, Elizabeth's own brothers and sisters, along with her children, visited Mr. and Mrs. Parra every day. Sam liked to watch Mr. Parra work in the yard, and to ask him questions. On Christmas eve, Mrs. Parra brought over presents for Sam and Annie, and on Valentine's Day she arrived with candy and cards. I began to feel the celebrated warmth, continuity, and strength of New Mexico's Hispanic families reaching out to touch our geographically manic, Anglo nuclear family.

The geographical proximity and emotional closeness of Elizabeth, her siblings, her parents, and her children exemplify what scholars have called "Chicano familism," which sociologists Maxine Baca Zinn and Stanley Eitzen define as "values emphasizing the family as opposed to the individual." This isn't to say that such families are without conflict or tension— just that they tend to hang together, to adapt to changing circumstances, and to be valued for concrete as well as abstract reasons. Elizabeth and her family represent some patterns typical of modern Chicano families, patterns including her own divorce (despite her devout Catholicism), her head-of-household status, and her employment in a white-collar, service-sector job. Her parents helped her bring up her children; as the Parras age, she and her siblings are taking care of them. But Elizabeth's kin also represent the optimistic end of the spectrum for Hispanic families. Her parents are able to live comfortably, if not opulently, on her father's pension, and to own their own home. They are in good health. Unlike most female heads

Children playing in front of a house in Professor Scharff's Neighborhood. Photo by Jon Hunner.

of households, particularly Chicana single mothers, Elizabeth makes a living wage. Her children, soon to be college graduates all, are ambitious and upwardly mobile: more American Dream stuff, New Mexico style.

Professor Scharff's Neighborhood, middling though it is, is by no means representative of New Mexico families. Telling you about the people I live near will reveal nothing, for example, about the dilemmas of New Mexico's poor, who were more than 17 percent of the state's population in 1979. Still, my neighbors' households tell us something about the current state of the American Dream, a normative conception of middle-class family life forged during the 1950s, a period by all demo-graphic accounts best understood as anomalous in American family history. You could go up and down our block and not find a single household that would conform to the pattern Americans enshrined as a family ideal on 1950s television shows, with a breadwinner father, homemaker mother, two children, one job, no divorces, no surprises. Across the street from us live an Anglo couple with two teenagers. They come pretty close to the "Leave It to Beaver" model. He's a retired career military man, now working in the defense business, the primary wage earner. Still, she works as a teacher. An older couple, who often take care of their three-year-old grandson, live next door to them, on one side. On the other, a divorced working mother (she's a health-care professional) lives with her teenage son. Most people in the neighborhood own their homes; a few rent. There are Anglo and Hispanic families. There are numerous elderly people—couples, widows, widowers, divorced people. There are families with young children too, buying into the neighborhood as the original owners age. On our block, the two other families with small children both include mothers on their second marriages. Older half-siblings and step-siblings are sometimes resident, and sometimes live with their fathers. And so, if you're looking for the Cleavers in my neighborhood, I fear you'll search in vain.

This excursion into my neighborhood is intended to make the point that there is not now, nor has there ever been, such a thing as "the family" in New Mexico. I know that the word *diversity* turns to dust in the mouths of political conservatives nostalgic for some mythical time when native-born and immigrant Americans leapt into a population porridge kettle eager to be stirred down to a molten mush. Whatever the kinship patterns of these different groups of people, all were supposed to end up conforming to a narrowly defined ideal family life. But *diversity* is a precise and useful term for characterizing both historical and contemporary families of New Mexico. Even in the space of one block of a middling Albuquerque neighborhood, where the seeming uniformity of the population is expressed architecturally in houses of roughly equal size and value, households and their inhabitants' relations to one another vary in obvious regards. The emotional, subjective, and even practical dimensions of those relations, and the material well-being of those inhabitants, may vary still more, and still be familial to the core.

What all this means is that understanding New Mexico families will mean putting this description of family life based on personal experience and observation in the context of broader social developments, while at the same time accounting for the varied and subjective ways in which families meet the challenges of contemporary life. What, then, do we know about changes in New Mexico families' lives in the past fifty years? And how might people have coped with these changes?

Let me offer some fairly obvious and general observations, the kinds of things most people understand intuitively, which are borne out by statistical information. To begin with, during the period between 1940 and 1990, the population of New Mexico has tripled, from 531,818 to 1,515,069. New Mexico has also urbanized and suburbanized. In 1940, only 176,401 New Mexicans, about one-third of all state residents, lived in places with populations over 2,500. The population of Albuquerque at that time was 35,449, roughly the same as present-day Laramie, Wyoming. By 1950, the population of New Mexico had grown to 681,187; by that time, 341,889 people, or 50.2 percent of New Mexicans were living in urban areas. By 1990, Bernalillo County alone had 480,577 residents, almost as many as the entire state had had fifty years earlier. In the interim, numerous suburban places (Rio Rancho, for example) had come into existence.

What do urbanization and suburbanization mean to people in post-World War II New Mexico? They mean lots of objective things, including changes in the landscape, and in the means by which we navigate the spaces in which we live. In California, of course, urbanization has taken a megalopolitan form, so that people who live in greater Los Angeles, for instance, often find themselves having to endure commutes of an hour or more each way as part of the cost of living and working. New Mexico is not, of course, California, but we would do well to take stock of the degree to which Californication has penetrated our borders. New Mexico culture is car culture. Our roadscapes—Route 66, Cerrillos Drive—tell much about us as urban people. Santa Fe, our City Different, is in one sense the City Generic writ large; it has *the nation's* highest per-capita incidence of fast-food restaurants. We may despise the form of architecture I have come to call "Pizza Hut Moderne," but mobile, working parents have certainly come to rely on Happy Meals and pepperoni pizzas as resources for feeding the family.

Albuquerque is a city growing on the Los Angeles model. We live in single-family dwellings and low-density neighborhoods, travel mostly on increasingly crowded arterial freeways and, infrequently and with difficulty, on minimal public transportation. Our rush-hour traffic reporters have become local celebrities. Our real estate developers dream of "planned" bedroom communities that would exacerbate urban sprawl by excluding commercial development (whether for offices, factories, or day-care centers) and by making driving, driving, and driving a more and more time-consuming necessity for working people.

Our cities sprawl as they expand, without benefit of much in the way of public transit. Private automobiles are our main form of transportation; the carless are at a substantial disadvantage. In 1980, only 38,442 New Mexicans reported using public transportation to get to work; 378,719, nearly ten times as many, traveled to work in private vehicles, and of those, 292,001 drove alone. As of 1980, mean travel time to work for

Albuquerque's skyline reflects the complexity of modern life in New Mexico. Photo by Jon Hunner.

New Mexicans ranged between sixteen and twenty-two minutes, a number far below the mean times for larger cities, but certainly reflecting urban growth.

Urban historians, demographers, and transportation planners must learn to recognize that the popular commitment to increasing time in the car cannot be measured in travel time to work alone. Social historians have identified the separation of home and workplace, which accompanied the industrial revolution, as a critical development in American families' history. I believe we need to start talking about the spatial *dispersal* of families that has accompanied metropolitanization. A family of four today may well inhabit four or more different places in the course of an ordinary day. Reassembling the family unit, as a practical matter of negotiating time and space, has become an increasingly complicated task. At the simplest level, trips to grocery stores and schools and child-care centers have become part of the practical equation for New Mexico families, although we have yet to adjust our notions of city planning to this spatial and temporal reality.

If urbanization has spawned a reliance on the automobile, which can be construed as both access to independent mobility and dependence on a wasteful, polluting means of transportation, cities also offer their inhabitants greater access to other forms of technology that affect family life. In 1940, 41.5 percent of habitable dwellings in the state as a whole had no running water. Statewide, 20.5 percent of dwellings had no running water within fifty feet of the dwelling. Among urban dwellings in 1940, however, only 19.8 percent had no running water. Indoor plumbing accompanied city building. By 1950 only 7.5 percent of urban households lacked running water, and in the state as a whole 20.4 percent of households had no indoor plumbing. That year, 82.5 percent of urban households had kitchen sinks. Some may object that indoor plumbing is a bourgeois convenience, important chiefly in urban settings in which high-density living makes sanitation problematic. Nevertheless, no one would argue that abolishing the job of hauling water had no consequences for the (female) persons charged with doing domestic work.

These statistics about the dissemination of domestic technology translate into very real changes in the lives of New Mexico families. Urban women do not have to walk to wells or pumps and carry buckets over distances. That fact of life might have meant that New Mexico women spent less time in washing people, clothes, and household surfaces. Instead, it seems to have meant that housewives have been expected to, and have themselves striven to, wash more *often*. Generally speaking, new forms of domestic technology between 1920 and 1960 did not decrease the amount of time women spent doing housework, though they did change the character of the work, making it less physically onerous if not less psychologically and socially important. What has seemed to have affected women's housework is their labor-force status, a subject to which I shall return in a moment.

As with the matter of access to, and need for, new technology, urbanization also means that New Mexicans have greater access to and dependence upon formal education. New Mexicans now are attending elementary and high school longer, graduating more often, and going on to college in far greater proportions than they did in 1940. It remains true that those with the lowest rates of school attendance, and the fewest years in school, live in rural places, particularly among the Native American portion of the population.

Certainly, we can discuss the question of the value of formal schooling, particularly when state-funded and federally funded education has sometimes mandated training of dubious utility to poor people, or has sought at least as much to enact a repressive vision of assimilation as to teach skills. Still, I would argue that people who live in contemporary New Mexico can have more power over their lives by taking charge of the kind of information formal education can make available. And yet, though more New Mexicans are getting more schooling, New Mexico, sadly, lags behind most other states in the performance of its educational system. In 1980, 18.3 percent of all 16-to-24-year-olds in the state were not in school, and not high school graduates, placing New Mexico in the bottom ten states in that category. New Mexico schools were also crowded, with the state rated fortieth also in pupil-teacher ratio in 1980.

Education has become increasingly critical to New Mexicans because urbanization also forces people to rely more on cash, rather than land, to secure the necessities of life. Although the number of years spent in school does not translate neatly into dollar income or occupational mobility for workers (sex

and race are more powerful forces in determining earnings),
lack of schooling has a cost. In the years since 1940, New
Mexico has become more like the rest of the nation in terms of
the ways in which people make a living. Small-farm and ranch
production remain part of the state's economic picture, but a
diminishing part. Industrialization, and postindustrialization,
have reshaped life in our state.

In the years since World War II, American economic
growth has occurred primarily in jobs involving neither farming nor manufacturing. The prewar stereotype of the American
worker was a blue-collar male who held some kind of manufacturing job, skilled or unskilled. The steel worker, the auto
worker, the factory hand producing textiles in the south, or
canned hams in Chicago, captured the imagination of both
advocates and opponents of unionization. Union organizers
focused their energies on such workers, with substantial success, particularly in the 1930s. Most New Mexicans, in those
days, were not "workers" in this image, but, instead, farmers
and ranchers.

Then came the war, which, as historian Gerald Nash has
demonstrated, transformed economic and social life in the
western United States. Manufacturing came west, in a big way,
and so did bureaucracy. Defense contractors and installations
lured job seekers and generated consumer businesses catering
to, and employing, growing populations. The civilian and the
military, the diplomatic and domestic, were inextricably bound
in New Mexico's social development. The cold war rationale
for an arms race—to safeguard American families from Com-
munist aggression—had its own particular ironic spin in New
Mexico. We glimpse that irony in the story of Los Alamos. In
that paradigmatic place of Nuclear Age New Mexico, scientist
professionals saw, in the magnificent canyons and mesas, safe
places for children to grow up. And all the while, these paternal

protectors of Trinity's children were themselves strewing the lovely landscape with the most toxic substances manufactured, so far, by human hands. In postwar New Mexico, we have reinvented the categories of safety and danger.

The war also catalyzed a permanent change in the composition of the labor force, as married women, including mothers, answered the need for workers in war industries and paved the way for ever-increasing female participation in wage work. The trend toward women's work-force participation correlated with the enormous growth in jobs in clerical, service, sales, and technical fields. In 1940, 78.4 percent of New Mexico men over the age of fourteen were in the work force; 21.6 percent were not, including 10.7 percent who were in school. That year, 18.7 percent of New Mexico women over the age of fourteen were in the labor force; 81.3 percent were not. Their rate of school attendance exactly matched that of men over fourteen, at 10.7 percent. 62.2 percent of women over fourteen were listed as "engaged in own home housework" (and, I might as well mention, 0.5 percent of men were listed as "engaged in own home housework").

By 1970, 74.0 percent of New Mexico men over the age of sixteen were in the labor force, indicating a very slight decline in male work force participation accounted for, possibly, by the facts that some nonworking men were able to collect disability insurance, and that men's life expectancy (and pension benefits) had increased. New Mexico women's labor-force rates, on the other hand, had doubled in the thirty-year period, to 36.9 percent of all women over sixteen. At that time, some 29.7 percent of New Mexico women with children under the age of six were working for wages; among mothers of young children who were not married, 44.9 percent were working or looking for work. By 1980, almost forty thousand New Mexico mothers of children under six—42.5 percent of all mothers of preschool-

age children in the state—were in the labor force. More than
fifty-five thousand mothers of children between the ages of six
and seventeen (57.2 percent of the total) were also working or
looking for work.

In the past fifty years, the growth of bureaucracies like the
state government, the University of New Mexico, and the
national laboratories has provided jobs for women workers. Out
of 140,269 persons employed in New Mexico in 1940, only
15,443 were listed as "clerical, sales, and kindred workers."
Prophetically, of that number, more than a third—some 6,075—
were women, comprising the largest category of female employment, although the most female-dominated job category in
New Mexico in 1940 was domestic service, which employed
5,177 women and only 267 men. By 1970 the number of female
clerical workers had more than doubled. That year, some forty-
one thousand New Mexico women did clerical work, roughly
one-third of all women workers in the state. Women also had
entered service, sales, technical, and professional work in
substantial numbers. Their wages, however, lagged far behind
those of men in full-time occupations, with the average wage
for a full-time employed woman stagnating at roughly two-
thirds of that for the average full-time employed man.

It almost goes without saying that most New Mexico
fathers work for pay; that's expected. What is worth repeating
is that today most New Mexico mothers work for pay, whatever
the ages of their children. Axiomatically, this makes a difference in family life, raising a series of questions. Some of them
I have already discussed—the kinds of work women do, for
example. Others are more complicated or troubling. How do
families cope with the fact of maternal employment? Who does
the housework traditionally performed by women? Are men
taking on more household and parenting tasks now that women
are taking on more breadwinning? How are families coping

Albuquerque families are making increasing use of child care facilities. Photo by Jon Hunner.

with speeded-up schedules and diminishing leisure time? Are mothers and fathers and children adjusting with grace and ease to new daily responsibilities that fly in the face of deeply felt ideas about motherhood and fatherhood, about masculinity and femininity, and about the responsibilities and rewards of belonging to a family? Sociologist Arlie Hochschild has written, "We're in the middle of a social revolution," and she has sensitively explored the myriad ways in which working couples face new dilemmas, with no help from politicians or government agencies. Hochschild has contrasted, with painful vividness, the potential for emotional satisfaction that family life might hold, with the frustrations of children forced to live at their parents' frantic pace and the burdens of what so many contemporary parents experience as "the second shift" at the end of the wagework day.

Two-job families obviously have their problems, coping
with the strains of pursuing the American Dream in a changing
economic, geographical, and social landscape. But most married working mothers feel lucky compared to the growing
number of women raising children alone, a situation increasingly common for mothers, still quite rare for fathers. In 1980,
23.0 percent, or nearly one-quarter of New Mexico children,
lived in single-parent families. Single motherhood in itself is
not necessarily a personal or social problem, despite negative
media images and politicians' cynical or fatuous attempts to
hold welfare mothers responsible for the federal deficit. At the
very least, many women and their children are better off,
physically and psychologically, living on their own than in the
same household as an abusive man. But inadequate education
and job training, and low wages in female-dominated occupations mean that few women can earn enough to support themselves and their children in comfort. Moreover, holding any
kind of job generally requires that a mother have access to high-
quality, affordable child-care, a service available to all too few
Americans. Single mothers and their children are thus tragi-
cally likely to fall into poverty. They comprise the majority of
the poor in the United States today. New Mexico, shameful to
say, is among the nation's leaders in this regard. A Children's
Defense Fund report estimated that in the years between 1983
and 1987 the average annual number of poor children in New
Mexico was about 117,000. That meant that 27.5 percent of all
children in the state in the mid-1980s lived in poverty. New
Mexico ranked sixth from the top among all states and the
District of Columbia in child poverty.

Whether never wed or divorced, single mothers in New
Mexico, and their children, face heavy odds. New Mexico's
divorced mothers can expect no help from either their children's
fathers or the state. Fewer than 10 percent of mothers who

sought child-support enforcement in 1988 received even one payment (ranking New Mexico forty-third among states in child-support enforcement). Unmarried mothers have even less hope of receiving state help in claiming nongovernmental support. In 1988, nearly one-third of all babies born in New Mexico were born to unmarried mothers. More than 10 percent of all New Mexico babies that year were born to unmarried teenagers. New Mexico's particular cultural background provides some benefits for some single mothers, particularly for Native American and Hispanic women, in the form of extended family-support networks exemplified, in my neighborhood, by Elizabeth and her kin. Such families continue to mitigate the problems of single motherhood for some women and children, despite urbanization and increased geographical mobility. But not all teenage mothers can count on such assistance. Compelled in most instances to interrupt their education, and to choose between earning a living and taking care of their children, most teen mothers face challenges that can defeat even the most loving families.

Many New Mexico babies are in trouble even before birth. More than 45 percent of New Mexico infants in 1988 were born to mothers receiving no prenatal care during the first trimester of pregnancy, and more than 16 percent of babies that year were born to women who received no care or late care; these figures put New Mexico squarely at the bottom of the nation in prenatal care. Such statistics reflect the larger fact that too many New Mexico families have no health insurance in an era of skyrocketing medical costs. Nationwide, according to the federal General Accounting Office, Hispanics are far more likely than other Americans to lack health insurance. An uninsured illness or accident can quickly plunge a family from relative comfort into a state of emergency.

Children are at risk in New Mexico, as are children across

the nation, vulnerable to the difficulties and discontents of modern life. The Children's Defense Fund reported some horrifying statistics last year. In the United States in 1991, every thirty-five seconds a baby was born into poverty. Every fourteen minutes an infant died in the first year of life. Every fourteen hours a child younger than five was murdered. Every day, 135,000 children went to school carrying guns. Every night, 100,000 homeless children sought a place to sleep. Every month, at least 56,000 children were abused. And that year, nearly half a million youths gave up and dropped out of school—one every ten seconds of the school day.

We live in a nation, and a state, where all too many children are left exposed to poverty, neglect, and danger. Albuquerque is not Los Angeles, where the murders of children have become so commonplace that people seem somehow numb to the mass tragedy. But neither is it a safe place for many of its children. One way or another, these imperiled, breathing human beings will seek someone to care for them and some way to express their sadness and rage. Their tragic lives spill out at us from our morning newspapers. Consider, for example, the story of fourteen-year-old Clarence "Peewee" Kennedy, who, in January 1992, fired a shotgun into a crowd of high school students standing outside a Blake's Lota Burger fast-food restaurant in Albuquerque, critically injuring another fourteen-year-old. "These things just happened," Kennedy explained to an interviewer shortly after the incident. "But when you're in a gang, that kind of stuff happens." For Clarence Kennedy, his gang offered more protection, more satisfaction, and more pleasure than his family life could ever afford. "No matter what I do or what I say," he said, "I'm always going to be from my gang. I ain't never going to forget where I come from." He was afraid, however, to return from the state juvenile-detention facility to

Albuquerque, where his mother lived. Rival gang members, he said, wanted revenge for the shooting.

Living, as we do, in a state that reveres the memory of Billy the Kid, it is wrongheaded, and perhaps self-righteous, to dwell overmuch on the deviance, or even the novelty, of Peewee Kennedy. But it is worth asking whether we can live with adolescent violence now, if indeed we ever could. Can we live in a world where gangs—"These things just happen"—replace families as nurturing institutions for poor children? Where even affluent families feel stretched, often to the breaking point, by the very facts of getting through the day? Where maintaining the nurturant, pleasurable dimensions of family life elude so many, and such diverse, New Mexicans?

The family may *never* have lived up to the ideal of being, in Christopher Lasch's wishful phrase, a "haven in a heartless world." But should we give up dreaming of a society that enables people to forge, and rely upon, bonds of affection? Politicians who insist that they are "pro-family" are assuredly responding to a widespread sense that the past fifty years has brought about a decline in Americans' ability to sustain satisfying family life. And yet, while the remarks I have made here demonstrate my own concern about challenges facing New Mexico's varied families today, I am not prepared to state, unequivocally, that more people had happy families fifty years ago than they do now. Indeed, our desire to return to some fictional golden age of the family, to reverse a purported historical decline, may be one of the most formidable barriers to solving the problems New Mexico's contemporary families encounter.

Attempts to impose conformity, to speak of "family" in the singular rather than acknowledge the strengths and problems of real and varied "families" in the plural, have been wrongheaded at best, pernicious at worst. Yet both "the family" and families themselves have always been contested terrain and have often focused political conflict in New Mexico. The image of the independent and happy fifties family—a family that survived and prospered on loyalty, discipline, and moral fiber without state "interference" or crippling federal "handouts"—is a myth that ignores the importance of such immense 1950s federal welfare programs as the G.I. Bill, which provided aid to veterans for college-education and home-purchase loans. Nostalgia for this make-believe family has nonetheless shaped recent public policy regarding American family life in both the nation and the state.

In the past fifty years, the government of the state of New Mexico has issued only one report dealing with family life. This document, "The People Speak on Families," was published in 1981, as a report to then-Governor Bruce King by the Council for the New Mexico Conference on Families. That agency was created in response to a Carter-administration call for state initiatives as part of a White House Conference on Families in 1980. The council, operating on a self-described "shoestring" budget, held hearings in different locations statewide, collected nearly one thousand pieces of testimony, conducted a state conference, and sent delegates to a meeting in Los Angeles.

Council members noted their desire to account for diversity among New Mexico families, to "examine the impact of economic and political forces related to poverty, unemployment, inflation and the energy crisis as they affect families in New Mexico," and to identify public policies "which may harm or neglect family life as well as . . . differing impact on particular groups, and to recommend new policies designed to strengthen and support families." These lofty goals are clearly based on a sense of urgency.

Such good intentions, to recognize families' diverse predicaments and to deal with them in a realistic manner, met up with the furious force of popular nostalgia on the road to the White House conference. When the time came to hold district hearings, self-styled "pro-family" groups representing the extreme wing of the New Right packed the meetings and dominated most of the recommendations reported out of both district and state gatherings. Thus, the state of New Mexico went on record with some rather interesting, and occasionally surreal, suggestions for meeting the complex and sometimes bewildering needs of contemporary American families. Confronting the question of how to define family at a time when New Mexico households often contained people unrelated by biology or by marriage, New Mexico took the position of trying to wish away all household groups that did not conform to a narrow definition of family. "The People Speak" report urged, "It should be the policy of the government to define the family as one of a relationship by heterosexual marriage, blood, or adoption." The report also suggested that the conference "strive to get laws to permit legal action against media for promoting other than heterosexual behavior."

When confronted with the predicament of the growing number of working mothers, New Mexico's representatives again narrowed discussion of an immensely complex and challenging contemporary social phenomenon, and put the significant question in the following fashion: "In what way do current policies on Equal Employment Opportunity harm the family?" They suggested a new system whereby heads of households would be given preferential treatment in hiring for all jobs, presumably as a means of keeping mothers out of the work force and in the home, thus disregarding the problems of thousands of New Mexico families dependent on two incomes. Faced with the growing need for good, affordable day care, the New Mexico conference officially opposed federal or state funding for day care.

The New Mexico conference's stated view on the issue of family violence reflected a longing for the bygone era of the "rule of thumb," when a man had the legal right to beat his wife and children with an instrument no bigger around than his thumb, without state interference. The official New Mexico position rejected any suggestion that government and society had an obligation to try to protect persons endangered by family members. Instead, the delegation asked, "How can we keep discipline of children outside of government and within the family?" Its answer: "Government should not support legislation that would infringe on parental rights of reasonable discipline."

Although the official positions adopted at district and state meetings clearly reflected the agenda of the New Right, the minority reports added to the document demonstrated the extent to which defining and supporting families lay at the heart of contemporary political battles. Some dismayed delegates, invoking "the ethnic diversity, cultural pluralism, and varying family values of New Mexico," submitted minority recommendations. A number of these minority reports took note of the challenges of varying family structures, the problems and possibilities created by geographical mobility, the horror of family violence, the demand for better child care, and the needs of working parents. For one set of conference participants, however, the majority report did not go far enough to warn against the dangers of such contemporary developments as maternal entry into the work force. These New Mexico citizens insisted that the important question facing the state in 1981 was "How can public education, government, and state and local agencies inform women [*sic*] of the adverse effects of pursuing a career outside the home on her and her family?"

I wonder whether we can become a people sufficiently fair and imaginative to try to seek real solutions to the problems that families of all kinds face? I am one of the lucky ones. I am a denizen of Professor Scharff's neighborhood and a citizen of New Mexico. I enjoy the privileges of affluence, the rewards of a fascinating job, the joys of living in the American West, and the love of my family. I would like to believe that through love and understanding, and the material support our two incomes provide, my husband and I can provide our children with the security and self-esteem they will need to cope with a world that seems so often determined to live up to Lasch's description as "heartless." We New Mexico families are diverse, but we depend on each other. We are neighbors, fellow citizens, sharing a powerful government that can do good or evil, and a fragile landscape that can be beautiful and humane, or ugly and hostile. We don't yet see our common interest. We haven't fully realized the promise of a heritage of familism. We are not yet family. Seeking some form of safety, we are reinventing danger.

A couple of weeks ago I noticed the slash of spray-painted gang graffiti on a building a couple of blocks from my house. The owners painted it over, but it soon reappeared, and every day there seemed to be one more nearby building subjected to the spray-can treatment. Sometimes, I believe, we need to admit that the handwriting is on the wall.

BIBLIOGRAPHY

In this essay, I have located my observations on New Mexico families in the context of discussions about the family in the post-World War II United States. Keeping in mind ethnic and class differences in family patterns, statistics garnered from decennial federal censuses suggest that New Mexico families usually reflect contemporary American trends in family living. What those trends mean, however, is subject to heated debate.

Sociologists, anthropologists, demographers, politicians, and political activists, in addition to historians, have addressed themselves to trying to understand family patterns in this period. We might designate their collective work as "postwar discourse on the American family." This discourse is large, varied, and politically charged, to say the least. Its subjects include such topics as the relative benefits or costs of mothers entering the work force, the problems and prospects of single-parent families, the rising rates of teenage pregnancy, the actual arrangements of power and of work in households, and the means by which families survive, fall apart, or regroup. A substantial portion of this literature is dense, jargon ridden, and technical. Another substantial portion reflects hidden or overt political agendas so extreme that the authors have abandoned all pretense of fairness in considering the evidence. For a guide to some of the most accessible, published work on the family in the twentieth-century American West, see Pat Devejian and Jacqueline J. Etulain, comps., *Women and Family in the Twentieth-Century American West: A Bibliography* (Albuquerque: Center for the American West, 1990).

My own perspective is shaped by fifteen years of research in women's studies, social history, urban history, and the history of technology. I have found most useful those studies which treat contemporary and historical families as complex, diverse, and fluid social groupings composed of individuals with sometimes divergent interests. Narratives that posit some past golden age of the family, when all Americans embraced a common vision of family life, when all family members joyfully subordinated their desires to the good of the group, when married parents resided together for their entire long lives, raised happy and obedient children, and peace and harmony reigned, are numerous, but historically inaccurate, and thus not very useful.

In 1971, sociologists Arlene Skolnick and Jerome Skolnick, members of the faculty at the University of California at Berkeley, recognized the history of diversity in family life, and assembled a suggestive collection of essays on the past, present, and future of families. *The Family in Transition: Rethinking Marriage, Sexuality, Child Rearing, and Family Organization* (Boston: Little, Brown, 1971) provides a sampling of informed opinion about sex, gender, and the family during a period of rapid, and sometimes frightening, social change.

For readers seeking a comprehensive and readable introduction to the myriad issues that families contain and confront, I recommend Maxine Baca Zinn and Stanley Eitzen, *Diversity in Families*, 2d ed. (New York: Harper and Row, 1990). This book includes an up-to-date and exhaustive bibliography that will help readers pursue specific interests.

Contemporary sociologists have produced perceptive studies of the day-to-day work that modern families must do to maintain themselves, particularly given the entry of mothers into the paid work force and the growth and decentralization of cities. Among the most insightful and engaging are Marjorie L. DeVault, *Feeding the Family: The Social Organization of Caring as Gendered Work* (Chicago: University of Chicago Press, 1991); and Arlic Hochschild, with Anne Machung, *The Second Shift* (New York: Avon Books, 1989).

A number of scholars have attempted to discover the impact of postwar feminism on American families, and on the adults and children that comprise families. Sociologist Sanford M. Dornbusch and economist Myra H. Strober, both on the faculty at Stanford University, administered a Ford Foundation grant to research perceived conflict between feminist agendas and children's interests, and in 1988 they edited a collection of essays, including policy recommendations, entitled *Feminism, Children, and the New Families* (New York: Guilford Press, 1988). Readers interested in issues including divorce, single-parent families, stepfamilies, child care, and government family policy will find this a useful collection.

The question of government policy has spawned studies of the family ranging from the sublime to the astounding. The Urban Institute, a Washington policy research and educational organization, addressed the question of government family policy in a politically careful volume, *The Changing American Family and Public Policy*, ed. Andrew Cherlin (Washington: The Urban Institute Press, 1988). The state of New Mexico, responding to a Carter-administration call for participation in a White House Conference on Families, produced in 1981 the slim but polemical report of the Council for the New Mexico Conference on Families. "The People Speak on Families: Report to the Governor," issued by the state in February 1981, details policy recommendations adopted at a statewide conference in Albuquerque. Reflecting the New Right political and social agenda of the group that packed the public meeting, the report is instructive reading for anyone who thinks participation in formal politics no longer matters.

Clearly, contemporary families face dilemmas not anticipated in the era of the so-called modern family, an anomalous but culturally powerful family form enshrined in the politics and popular culture of 1950s America. In the mid-1980s, sociologist Judith Stacey spent months in interviewing two working-class family groups living and struggling with postindustrialization in California's Silicon Valley. Stacey's gripping and sensitive study of these two "postmodern" families, *Brave New Families: Stories of Domestic Upheaval in Late Twentieth Century America* (New York: Basic Books, 1990), is must reading for anyone interested in American families today.

FIVE

ETHNICITY

COOPERATION AND CONFLICT IN MODERN NEW MEXICO AS REFLECTED IN LITERATURE AND ART

ROSALIE OTERO

CONTEMPORARY New Mexican culture is a result of four hundred years of interaction among ethnic groups. The traditions and cultures are as variable as the landscape. This is especially evident in the curious merging of the modern and the historic as well as the cultural mixing of Anglo, Native American, Hispanic, African American, and other ethnic groups in the state. For example, the iconography in Pueblo churches associates Catholic saints and Indian symbols. A Los Alamos scientist attends the Shalako dances at Zuni, and a Native American rides an International Harvester, while a little northern Hispanic town sports neon signs advertising "Bud Light." The multiple languages and dialects, too, have diversified and crossbred. Only in New Mexico do we have *"trocka"* and *"lonche."*

The reality that is New Mexico is rooted in the collective experience that is multicultural and ethnically diverse. It grows out of and shapes our history, politics, culture, and literature. The issue of ethnicity in New Mexico is one of cooperation and conflict among cultures. Literature and art are both a reflection and a force. They may record a view of society—its values, problems, structure, events—and they may also influence the society. More often, literature and art embody the artists' evaluations of their world, or illuminate its possibilities.

For many New Mexicans, the coming of World War II brought a new awareness, an interchange of information and experience, and often a disillusionment, but, at other moments, a rebirth of pride. The Anglo-American value system and socioeconomic structure have caused tensions within ethnic communities. The dominant view in America is a combination of meritocracy and capitalism. An integral part of this view is the conviction that hard work and perseverance will be rewarded by success and that success is defined as wealth and economic status. This reality has not been true for many ethnic and immigrant Americans in New Mexico. Success, by and large, has meant relinquishing one's ethnic identity, having to choose between social networks, kinship ties, ritual, and tradition and the lure of upward mobility and material gain. For many groups, there remains a constant tension between ethnic loyalty and identification and the economic lure of homogenized mainstream American society. As a result, what emerges in the literature and the art are sometimes racial clichés and distorted caricatures rather than authentic voices. It becomes important, therefore, to underscore the importance and the legitimacy of the aesthetics of ethnicity in the study of New Mexico.

Ethnicity counts. It is significant on several levels. First, membership in a particular group is an integral part of self-identity, an important component of everyone's answer to the question "Who am I?" A group of people of the same race or national origins, speaking the same language and/or sharing a common and distinctive culture, is an ethnic group. Common racial identity alone does not characterize an ethnic group; a sharing of history and cultural tradition is required. Ethnicity may determine what you eat, what you wear to a funeral, when you celebrate a holy day, what career you plan for, whom you marry, where you live, and whom you choose as friends.

The El Dorado passive Solar Adobe Home combines traditional New Mexican charm with energy efficient technology. Photo by Mark Nohl. (Courtesy New Mexico Economic and Tourism Department.)

Ethnicity counts in other ways as well. It has become a focus for political organization. It can be a matter of lobbying and pressure groups, union membership, house availability, career opportunity, school-curriculum changes, and elections won or lost.

Minority-group members have often been accorded less than equal treatment, but especially in recent years ethnic groups have tended to respond to discrimination by a militant self-awareness—in a way, they are coming out of a collective identity crisis. Since the end of the Second World War, a new ethnic awareness has manifested itself. Never before have so many Americans asserted their distinctive group affiliations or formed study groups and more formal organizations to explore the meanings of their diverse origins and to put forward their claims on the public consciousness. Writers and speakers from

every conceivable background appear in magazines and newspapers and on television to call national attention to one issue
or another. On a daily-life level, people are exploring such
things as ethnic arts and crafts and authentic cookery. We are
enriched, though at times confused, by the ethnic variety that
surrounds us.

Minorities in the state are concerned not merely with
challenging the system that chooses to accord them a marginal
economic and social role, but with reexamining their own
system of values. The novel, short story, poem, painting, or
sculpture becomes an expression and sometimes a justification. The multiplicity of the state and its literary and artistic
production focuses on a view of New Mexico that is ethnic
identified, which is to say that it stresses an Americanness not
concerned with melting away differences into a pot of homoge-
neity, but one that, instead, seeks to foreground ethnicity—that
is, cultural distinctiveness—as an integral measure of individual and collective humanity.

New Mexico's literary tradition begins with the orally
transmitted myths, legends, and rituals of the Indians who were
native to the soil when the Spaniards came and who still inhabit
it. This literature, unrecorded until the nineteenth century,
extends far back in time and is still an integral feature of
contemporary literature. In her poem, "A Breeze Swept
Through," Luci Tapahonso incorporates the myths she grew up
with as well as her own experience of giving birth:

> The first born of dawn woman
> slid out amid crimson fluid streaked with stratus clouds
>   her body glistening August sunset pink
>   light steam rising from her like rain on warm
>   rocks

Leslie Marmon Silko, of Laguna, Mexican, and white ancestry, blends the cultures with mythology in her writing. In "The Man to Send Rain Clouds," we see two religious traditions, Christian and Laguna, coalesce in one moving ceremony. In her novel, *Ceremony* (1977), Silko again blends Laguna oral tradition with the struggles of Tayo, the protagonist. Before the white man entered the world, "the people shared the same consciousness." The story of the white people's arrival thus also describes the first knowledge of separation, the recognition of a rift in the unity and wholeness of things in both individual and communal experience. The nature of Tayo's dislocation and inner illness unfolds in the novel through two distinct narrative styles. One style forwards the present time of the story; the other relates the timeless traditional tales that comment on it.

Native American stories in prose may be classified as myths, legends, and folktales. The myths recount the deeds of gods, the divine ancients who founded religion or explained natural phenomena. The legends describe historic individuals who shaped tribal destiny by notable exploits. The folktales treat the familiar and humorous everyday world, frequently exploiting animal lore as a satire on wit and cunning wherever they are found.

Although Native Americans, particularly in the Southwest, date their occupancy in this area at about ten thousand years before Christ, Anglo authors, for the most part, have used the Indian as a stage prop, a background character. The myth of Pueblo life began when most of the artists and writers who had settled in the Taos and Santa Fe art colonies were critical of the world they had left behind. No matter how objective their analysis of Native American culture, it was filtered through a screen of discontent, of longing for a simpler, more fundamental way of life. The phenomenon, best described as a mild form of primitivism, conditioned Anglos to view Native American life in idyllic terms. Consequently, they reveal more about Anglo attitudes than they do about Indian life. By the 1920s, for example, in paintings Taos men were not likely to wear elaborate Plains leggings, but the image enabled Anglo artists to impose on Indian life the sense of order and harmony they themselves were seeking. Joseph Henry Sharp's painting *Crucita* portrays a Taos Indian girl in more authentic garb, albeit a Hopi wedding dress. But at her feet is an earthen bowl containing zinnias (not native to the Southwest) and a variety of other flowers. Such a floral arrangement would not have been part of an Indian household; in fact, the picture is an Anglo conceit, meant to advertise the aesthetic sensibilities of an Indian in a way that an Anglo audience could understand.

Fortunately (although one suspects rarely), Anglos in New Mexico could view themselves with humor, as writer Erna Fergusson revealed: "Everybody had a pet pueblo, a pet Indian, a pet craft. Pet Indians with pottery, baskets, and weaving to sell were seated by the corner fireplace, plied with tobacco and coffee, and asked to sing and tell tales."

Native Americans have known change throughout their ages-old history. But the tendency of historians, anthropologists, artists, and writers has been to treat Indian history as static. The changes Native Americans have experienced are considered exceptions to the norm. The variety inherent in all human life has not been considered.

Anglo writers with some exceptions still maintain patronizing attitudes when writing about the Native American. Irwin R. Blacker's novel, *Taos* (1959), depicts the period of Spanish rule in 1598 until the Pueblo Revolt in 1680. Blacker's story is history with special liberties to emphasize the ruthless nature of colonial administration. The lives of the characters, as presented in an imaginary pueblo called Santa Flora, offer sufficient motivation for Indians to revolt, but the morals as well as the cruelty challenge probability. William Eastlake's novels, *Go in Beauty* (1956), *The Bronc People* (1958), and *Portrait of an Artist with Twenty-six Horses* (1963), use an Indian reservation with a background of ranching that is realistic, but as the following excerpt from *The Bronc People* shows, names like My Prayer, Quicker-Than-You, President Taft, and Four Thumbs change the mood to caricature. Even the supposedly Indian names are not realistic:

> "Can you see all right?" the tall Indian asked. The tall Indian's name was President Taft.
> "Very well," the short Indian said. The short Indian allowed the trader to call him My Prayer. They both had Indian names, too—Water Running Underneath The Ground and Walking Across A Small Arroyo. They both wore hats and they had on army surplus shoes and they both rolled cigarettes without taking their eyes off the spectacle they were watching.

Luci Tapahonso, in her poem, "Hard to Take," points to the uncomfortable business of discrimination:

> Last week in Gallup,
> I was in line at Foodway
> one checkstand open and
> a long line of Navajos waiting
> . . . my turn and I fumble
> dropping my change
>   Sorry, I say, sorry.
>   The cashier looks up smiling
>   first smile in 20 minutes of Navajo customers
>   Oh—that's okay. Are you Navajo?

I swear, you don't have an accent at all!
. . . I say to the people behind me
Ha' 'at'iisha'ni?
Why is she saying that to me?
We laugh a little under our breaths
and with that
    I am another Navajo

In an earlier novel, *The Man Who Killed the Deer* (1942) by Frank Waters, Martiniano pleads before the Indian Council after killing a deer out of season:

The Council does not give me the privilege of others
since I have come back from away-school. It would not
give me my turn at the thresher for my oats, my
wheat. . . . Should I go without my rights for two days of
white man's law? The white man's Government that
took me away to school, for which you do not give me
the privileges of others? What is the difference between
killing a deer on Tuesday or Thursday? Would I not have
killed it anyway?

Harold Littlebird, a potter and poet from Laguna and Santo Domingo pueblos, contrasts the understanding of white anthropologists and Native American mystic wisdom in his poem, "For the Laughing Bear":

. . . I left the kiva
coming out into the wind again
. . . clouds parted and Father Sun told me you were listening
and a friend who was there with me laughed
at the way archeologists and professors of science
explain with signs on the ruin trail
the way my Grandfathers lived three hundred years ago

and we laughed with my Grandfathers
all the way to the car on the first day of spring

N. Scott Momaday, in his novel *House Made of Dawn*
(1968), also writes about the Native American's ancient heritage and long tenure in this state:

> The people of the town have little need. They do not
> hanker after progress and have never changed their
> essential way of life. Their invaders were a long time in
> conquering them; and now, after four centuries of
> Christianity, they still pray in Tanoan to the old deities
> of the earth and sky and make their living from the
> things that are and have always been within their reach;
> while in the discrimination of pride they acquire from
> their conquerors only the luxury of example. They have
> assumed the names and gestures of their enemies, but
> have held on to their own, secret souls; and in this there
> is a resistance and an overcoming, a long outwaiting.

Some Anglo writers, however, have portrayed Native
Americans in a more realistic, less patronizing manner. Alice
Marriott's *María, The Potter of San Ildefonso* (1948) is a realistic biography about the daily life in the pueblo and the work of
María. Another successful writer, Tony Hillerman, writes
mystery stories that also treat Native Americans as real people.
In *The Blessing Way* (1970), for example, murder mars the
serenity of the cliffs and caves of the Anasazi before the mystery
is solved. In this novel, Lt. Joe Leaphorn, a college-educated
Navajo policeman, uses his knowledge of ancient ways as an
advantage in solving modern crimes.

Kirk Gittings (photographer) and V. B. Price (poet), in their
recent book *Chaco Body* (1991), capture the beauty and heritage
of a place and a people with profound sensitivity and wonder:

Never freed from now,
I cannot hear them,
      I can have
         no memory of their lives.
            Their voices are behind me
      even though I am
         what they have left behind.

Judy Wells, in her poem "Navajo Women," draws on the realities of radiation cancer on the Navajo population working in the uranium mines in Grants and focuses on the strength of the women:

Purple, turquoise
and red figures
are moving down the hill
They sit in clusters
the old women
listening to speeches . . .
Why do I
in faded blue
jeans
keep staring at those
Navajo women
as if they held the secret
in their jewel-like
skirts and shirts . . .

In her short story "Flute Song," Patricia Clark Smith describes the setting and characters in unsentimental yet vivid prose. In this short excerpt, Carol, an Anglo woman and new to New Mexico, is invited for Matachines, a fiesta at the Jemez Pueblo:

The pueblo lay in a hollow just before the road started to climb into the Jemez mountains. One and two story

adobes clustered against a big background of red cliffs
and chalky tent rocks, like pillars of salt. They parked
near the trading post and followed the sound of chanting
down to a central plaza lined with people, Anglo and
Indian. More Indians sat on the roofs, teen-age boys
mostly. No one seemed especially reverent. Children
raced around, and in front of her two old women in
flowered house dresses and bright patterned shawls sat
in green and white plastic chairs, talking in English
about the bad luck of somebody named Willy. The air
smelled sharply of wood smoke and frying dough.

The 1930s saw some dramatic changes in federal Indian
policy. Under the guidance of John Collier, commissioner of
Indian affairs from 1933 to 1945 and architect of the Indian New
Deal, Indian policy veered away from the assimilationism of
the previous decades. But the years after World War II marked
a pendulum swing back toward assimilationist education and
a society less accepting of cultural diversity.

Indian veterans who returned to the Southwest had employment experience in the defense industry. They had gained
new insights and knowledge, but once again they were faced
with prejudice and neglect. The English-only policy was rein-
troduced in schools. And in the spirit of assimilation, activities
for Native Americans duplicated those of the Anglo communities, such as 4-H clubs and Boy Scouts.

Raquel Montoya describes the experience of becoming
assimilated in her poem, "Unweaving My Tongue":

I, too, am of mixed race.
I understand the hatred
inherent in that loving. . . .
I grow slowly
in Spain and England

I learn to speak aristocratic English, Castilian Spanish.
Birthdays bring packages from Isleta
books, Knowing Your Indian Heritage,
turquoise crosses I never wear
. . . I learn to sit Indian-style,
to be ashamed of savage red Indians,
heretical medicine men.
I am asked why my skin is brown
why my eyes are black.
    I learn to lie . . . .
    My mind is coming home.
I have swept my Indian beneath my White.

The rise of ethnic studies programs in minority-group history and literature did not always do justice to ethnic groups. Educators felt that if they stressed the positive aspects of a group they had solved the major problems of that group in its relation to the rest of society. Emphasizing that black is beautiful or that Native Americans have contributed the names of rivers and lakes is insufficient.

The 1970s ushered in an affirming policy of self-determination. Significant reform legislation affecting Native Americans was passed. Native Americans themselves have moved toward control of all aspects of their lives. They have begun to pay artistic attention to their own realities. There is a growing trend among creative people of Indian heritage to pursue careers in the arts that are not defined or restricted by tradition. Fritz Scholder and R. C. Gorman, for example, are internationally known artists. Scholder possesses a strong feeling for the dramatic and always shuns the old spirit of imitation. His bold disregard of traditions enables him to wrought powerful changes in composition. He feels honored when he is told that he has destroyed the traditional style of Indian art. Scholder startled many people by not portraying the Indian as many Anglo

New Mexico artist Mary Ann Nibbelink's rendering of traditional garb in Indian Headdress. *(Courtesy* New Mexico Magazine's *1992 Distinguished Artists Calendar.)*

painters had done. Scholder paints twentieth-century Indians doing twentieth-century things. R. C. Gorman, on the other hand, is more traditional, less startling, but, nevertheless, original. His childhood was dominated by his mother, his great-grandmother, and his maternal grandmother, whom he credits with introducing him to beauty and to his Navajo heritage.

Other Native American artists and writers also have begun to express their individuality and ethnicity. Among the values they stress in their work are a sense of the sacredness and unity of nature, an awareness of our relatedness to other animals, a sense of the spiritual inherent in the material, and of the mystery and appropriateness of life. Native American values tend toward the unaggressive and affiliative rather than the achievement oriented. Some artists working in a variety of mediums include Herman Agoyo, a native of San Juan Pueblo;

Louis Baca, a member of the Santa Clara Pueblo, but raised on the Jicarilla Apache reservation; Lena Carr, a Navajo and independent producer of video and films; La-Verne Garcia, a Cochiti and San Juan Pueblo native; Tommy Edward Montoya, a painter, poet, and narrator of San Juan Pueblo; Laura Fragua, a Jemez abstract sculptor; Nora Noranjo-Morse, a poet from Santa Clara Pueblo; and Swazo Hinds of Tesuque Pueblo. As Paula Gunn Allen, a Laguna native, says:

> The tribes seek through song, ceremony, legend, sacred
> stories (myths), and tales to embody, articulate, and
> share reality, to bring the isolated self into harmony
> and balance with this reality, to verbalize the sense of
> the majesty and the reverent mystery of all things, and
> to actualize, in language, those truths of being and
> experience that give to humanity its greatest signifi-
> cance and dignity. The artistry of the tribes is married to
> the essence of language itself, for in language we seek to
> share our being with that of the community, and thus to
> share in the communal awareness of the tribes.

The distinct Native American awareness of self is of necessity influenced by technological "progress" and change, which are irreducible, and one must either surmount them or be buried under them. The machine and, now, the computer have invaded New Mexico, and it will not do simply to shut one's eyes and pretend they are not there. Paula Gunn Allen in her poem, "Kopis'taya" (A Gathering of Spirits) writes about this contemporary reality:

> We are women of daylight; of clocks and steel foundries,
> of drugstores and streetlights, of superhighways that
> slice our days in two. Wrapped around in glass and steel
> we ride our lives. . . .

Simon Ortiz, known primarily for his poetry, published *Fightin'*, a book of short stories in 1983. One of the stories in the collection, "Men on the Moon," is an account of the 1969 moon landing told from the point of view of an old Indian man. Through the old man's naïveté and confusion, Ortiz questions the wisdom of the people who undertake moon shots in their quest for knowledge while ignoring much of what they should know about life on earth:

> Are those men looking for something on the moon? he asked his grandson.
> They're trying to find out what's on the moon, Nana, what kind of dirt and rocks there are, to see if there's any life on the moon. The men are looking for knowledge, Amarosho told him.
> Faustin wondered if the men had run out of places to look for knowledge on the earth. Do they know if they'll find knowledge? he asked.

Native American writers have written about the death of entire civilizations. Leslie Silko, in her novel *Ceremony* (1977), for example, sees the bomb as an enigma, as both the creation and the potential source of the destruction of the culture that made it.

> From that time on, human beings were one clan again,
> united by the fate the destroyers planned for all of them,
> for all living things; united by a circle of death that
> devoured people in cities twelve thousand miles away,
> victims who had never known these mesas, who had
> never seen the delicate colors of the rocks which boiled
> up their slaughter.

Native American artists and writers are forcing us all to reevaluate the Indians and their part in the New Mexican

Elias Rivera's Indian Market *captures the excitement of Santa Fe's annual Native American Arts and Crafts Fair. (Courtesy* New Mexico Magazine's *1992 Distinguished Artists Calendar.)*

experience. It is proof that the Navajos, Apaches, and nineteen Pueblo communities in New Mexico have not vanished and that they, too, add dimension, heritage, and cultural diversity to our state. While the trappings may have changed—for example, men now drive in pickup trucks to ceremonials—the essence of Native American life seems to survive.

In the sense of the written or printed word, New Mexican literature began with the old Spanish chronicles of exploration and conquest. These basic sources of history rank among the great original adventure books of the world. In human interest and genuine literary flavor, these straightforward tales of priests, conquerors, and soldiers seem today as fresh and modern as when they were written. Another phase of early Spanish literature in New Mexico is represented in the religious plays, traditional songs, ballads, and folk tales brought from Spain and still extant among the descendants of the early colonists, as evidenced in such works as *Abuelitos: Stories of the Río Puerco Valley* (1992), collected and edited by Nasario García.

The regular arrival of Anglo-Americans in New Mexico had dramatic economic and cultural impact on the indigenous Hispanic people. A once relatively self-sufficient culture sustained by a local system of barter, and augmented by commerce with Mexico, increasingly gave way to a mercantile system dependent on the exchange of cash for goods. Traditional means of keeping food on the table crumbled as grazing and farm lands were lost to federal forest reserves and Indian land claims. Hispanics increasingly found themselves depending on seasonal work away from home or competing for jobs where abundant cheap labor precluded a power to negotiate reasonable wages.

More significant to Hispanic life, Anglos assumed the position of the principal culture in New Mexico and, since they were enamored of Pueblo customs more than Hispanic, relegated the numerically and once culturally dominant Hispanic population to lowest status among these three groups. Jimmy Santiago Baca expresses this concept in strongest terms:

> I believe there was violent, violent attempt by the authorities to bleed the Chicanos and the Indios and the Mestizos of any identity, any cultural remnants. There was a really strong effort at that, a most sophisticated effort. It was not outright "Let's go out and shoot them"; it was, "Let's do it through education, let's do it through religion, let's bleed these people so they haven't got nothing left, so their only alternative is to become who we want them to become." And they accomplished that to a certain degree.

Originally, Hispanic crafts in colonial New Mexico grew out of the need to provide Catholic churches and missions, family chapels, and homes with both devotional objects and furnishings. Beginning about 1790, local image-makers created the religious icons. Their carved and painted figures that were of imposing scale and emotional expressiveness, included, for example, cadaverous- skinned, bleeding saviors on black crucifixes. Sacred images painted on flat, wood *retablos*, or carved in three-dimensional figures called *bultos*, were made by local artisans whose style and skills were provincial reflections of the artistic traditions of Renaissance Spain and colonial New Mexico. As traditions deepened and broadened, the chests, chairs, benches, and tables of woodcarvers, the floor coverings and blankets of weavers, and later the candle sconces and tin *nichos* came to have a decorative style that was recognizably Hispanic New Mexican: strong but simple design and form, bold color and pattern, and relatively unsophisticated craftsmanship.

With the opening of the Santa Fe Trail in 1821, however, factory-made products began to replace handcrafted home furnishings, and mass-produced plaster statuary replaced religious objects. Eventually, however, the local arts and crafts became popular with collectors and curio-shop owners. Every *bulto* and *retablo* that could be found was snatched up with great enthusiasm, and Hispanic artists were encouraged to carve and paint in the "old way." The disjuncture between artistic enthusiasm and day-to-day reality, between what was painted and what was actually experienced, and between consciously stated and unconsciously held attitudes, however, manifested itself in negative stereotyping. Perhaps there was no single way in which Anglos deflated Indian or Hispanic cultures more than by reducing them to tourist mementos.

Beyond reducing historical and religious objects to entertaining trifles, some denigrated Hispanic culture by class stereotypes. Popular writers often cast their imaginative conceptions of the Hispanic poor in less than flattering terms. Harvey Fergusson introduced Ramón Delcasar, the central character in *The Blood of the Conquerors* (1936), as someone who had frequently encountered racial slurs: "But his social footing was a peculiarly uncertain thing for the reason that he was a Mexican. This meant that he faced in every social contact the possibility of a more or less covert prejudice against his blood, and that he faced it with an unduly proud and sensitive spirit concealed beneath a manner of aristocratic indifference."

Often, the Anglo wrote rhapsodically of New Mexico. Grandiloquent prose and poetry may have sprung from authentic and unique features of New Mexican life, but there was a point at which enthusiastic language robbed the layered cultures of their complexity and made them appear poorer in ideas and history than they actually were.

Perhaps no perception of Hispanics was more routinely drawn in the visual arts than that of the persevering laborer, fatigued by servitude to the land, but somehow able to find repose in mere subsistence. These images suggest an extremely passive people, mute in contemplation of their fate, yet made heroic by their struggle to survive. Image after image depicted individual figures, usually elderly, sitting or standing with drooped shoulders, bowed head, and gnarled, worn hands that show strength but not energy. Kenneth Adams's *Evening*, Emil Bistram's *Comadre Rafaelita*, and Ernest Blumenschein's *The Plasterer* depict Hispanics as wooden, staring with unseeing eyes, worn.

For many Hispanic artists, on the other hand, art is essentially an avenue of social protest. It is an art that reflects the greatness and sacrifices of the past, an art that clarifies and intensifies the present desires of a people who will no longer be taken for granted as second-class citizens. The art often serves

as a shield to preserve and protect the cultural values. Bernadette
Rodriguez's *El Trabajador*, for example, shows both strength
and vitality. Rosa María Calles's work also displays an in-
tensely personal and poetic revelation of Hispanic New Mexico.
"I want to make a visual statement that tells a story about the
hardships, trials, tribulations, sorrows and joys of my people,"
she says. Ray John de Aragon reinforces the magic and timeless
mood in a culture that firmly believes in a mystic spirituality.
He says, "I feel it is imperative that the Hispanic culture of New
Mexico be represented factually on canvas and recorded truth-
fully in print." Amado Maurilio Peña's work is filled with
images that reflect a spiritual bond with the Native American
culture. His paintings are colorful and portray his keen observations of a land and its people, a molding of his Hispanic and
Indian heritage. Guillermo Martínez Augustine's art, on the
other hand, is dark, often horrific. Religion, deformity, frustra-
tion, authority figures, politics, and unspoken evils are his
subjects. Some Hispanic artists express their ethnicity with
emotionally vibrant murals taking up whole walls. Enriqueta
Vásquez, a prolific writer and painter says, "Each mural is a
learning process. But ideas are there; ideas from way down deep
come out in a paint brush. What you want to say to people is
very important. As an artist you have an obligation to the
people." After she designs and organizes a mural, she invites
other people to come and paint. "I like other people to come.
After all it's their mural and why shouldn't it be their experience. However they paint, I respect it. And after it's done, you
get a mural with different hands, different hearts, all complete
as one."

In the hands of Anglo artists portraying Hispanics, the land
was not always providential; it was a test to be met, a trial to be
endured, a source of tribulation and bare survival. Hispanic

artists, on the other hand, describe the land with intensity and reverence. Richard Sandoval's *Nambe River* and *The Sandias* are two watercolors that depict his connection to the land. Rudolfo Anaya makes the landscape around the children's hospital in his novel *Tortuga* (1979) symbolic of hope: "And even though the rest of the landscape alternates between the dead desert with the sandstorms and the frozen mountains on the west side, the springs of the mountain are still running—there is still hope, it's not too late, and you can go there and you can bathe and be made whole."

The artist's perception of Hispanics did not derive solely from the themes of land and labor. The Roman Catholic church was the most apparent backdrop to much of New Mexican life, and this fact is evident in the images. Georgia O'Keeffe's painting of crosses, particularly those that fill the canvas, figure as stark evidence of the demanding presence of Catholicism in New Mexico. Less iconic are still lifes with devotional objects, sunny views of rural churches, the dramatic scenes of Penitente rituals. B. J. O. Nordfeldt, *Still Life with Santo*, and Willard Nash's *Penitentes* are two examples.

By the end of World War II, the Anglo community was well established in New Mexico. The Anglo intellectuals, writers, and artists who came to New Mexico invented an aesthetic discourse of myth and romance that deeply inscribed itself upon the popular consciousness. Along with the discursive form came an entire structure of troubling assumptions about native Hispano culture, history, language, and the self.

Charles F. Lummis's widely read *The Land of Poco Tiempo* (1893) may be identified as a significantly generative text and Lummis himself as a central agent of cultural invention. Focusing on the landscape at great length, as well as on the physiognomy and cultural practices of "the Mexican," "the Pueblo," and "the Apache," Lummis's book was a combination of sensational ethnography, impressionistic history, and amateur archaeology. His lyrical romance of the Southwest opens thus:

> Sun, silence, and adobe—that is New Mexico in three words. . . . Here is the land of *poco tiempo*—the home of "Pretty Soon." Why hurry with the hurrying world? The "Pretty Soon" of New Spain is better than the "Now! Now!" of the haggard States. The opiate sun soothes to rest, the adobe is made to lean against, the hush of day-long noon would not be broken. Let us not hasten— *mañana* will do. Better still, *pasado mañana*.

Later writers, however, employ a more realistic style. John Nichols's *Milagro Beanfield War* (1974), for example, is a convincing novel. He captures local color, customs, legends, beliefs, and geographical particularities with keen insight. This novel exposes a people's endless struggle against outside special-interest groups for land, water, and grazing rights. Frank Waters, in an earlier novel, *People of the Valley* (1941), is also realistic. He tells the story of a domineering *curandera* driven by customs and superstitions. The novel deals with many early traditions such as penitentes and communal life-styles, while the people struggle against a series of forces such as the church, government, nature, and Anglo "progress."

The changes that came about because of increasing population and "modernization" had a dramatic effect on the lives of Hispanics. E. A. Mares, in his short story "Florinto," captures the changes and the prevailing patronizing attitude as well as the resentment of the Hispanic community toward this attitude as well as the changes themselves:

> Another summer had come and gone, and then another and another, and after that I lost track of them. World

War II had ended and a trickle of tourists, soon to
become a flood, came to Albuquerque to visit Old Town.
About that time, the city decided to pave New York
Avenue and change its name to Lomas Boulevard, which
had a more authentic, native ring. A long dead tongue of
asphalt now ran from Old Town clear up into the
Heights at the other end of town. The Anglos who lived
in the Heights began to travel down the new road into
Old Town in ever large numbers. They would come in
their shiny cars and wearing their beautiful new clothes.
They would walk around he plaza, take pictures, visit
the San Felipe Church, and go to one of the restaurants
on the plaza where they would enjoy "authentic Spanish
food," which was really Indian and New Mexican food
prepared with a very mild chile sauce. They came, most
of all, to recreate in their minds a fantasy of the
"Spanish way of life," to confirm what they had seen in
countless Western movies, complete with real Indians
who sat around the plaza selling the jewelry they had
made. The merchants of the city moved quickly to take
advantage of the tide of money which poured into Old
Town. The Spanish-speaking families which had lived
there for centuries were shunted aside, forced by new
zoning laws and by economic pressure to move to the
poorer neighborhoods near the Río Grande.

In *The Last of the Menu Girls* (1986), Denise Chavez adds
real insight and a feminine voice to the human dimension of the
community. Through the eyes of Rocío Esquibel, the protagonist, we see characters that are rarely depicted in fiction: people
occupying a secondary plane as janitors, gardeners, and nurses'
aides. Chavez develops full characters who, despite their lowly
occupations, hold great truths.

The Hispanic poet often sees nature as teacher, and the

Albuquerque artist Betty Sabo depicts a winter scene in Twilight in Arroyo Seco.
(Courtesy New Mexico Magazine's *1992 Distinguished Artists Calendar.)*

process of identification with nature is a necessary means toward wisdom and knowledge. In Rudolfo Anaya's *Bless Me, Ultima* (1972), Antonio touches nature through Ultima: "When she came the beauty of the llano unfolded before my eyes, and the gurgling waters of the river sang to the hum of the turning earth. The magical time of childhood stood still, and the pulse of the living earth pressed its mystery into my living blood." The novel includes a rich weaving of myth and legend. Anaya implies a need for seeking a new way of life through an eclectical syncretism of experiences: "every generation, every man is part of his past. He cannot escape it, but he may reform the old materials, make something new."

Sabine Ulibarrí, in *Tierra Amarilla: Stories of New Mexico* (1971), relates early experiences in an isolated, rural-pastoral setting of northern New Mexico. The past is judged and relived as it produces a different emotion through the passing of time. In "Forge Without Fire," for example, Ulibarrí tells the story of Edumenio, a blacksmith who fixed broken toys and treated the children without condescension. Edumenio fell in love with a lovely woman named Henrietta, but the community scorned her because she was "one of those girls," so she left Edumenio. He, too, disappeared some years later.

> Years passed. The smithy went on deteriorating as all human artifacts must do. I am no longer nine years old. I am a man. But I remember and I weep. I am ashamed of human nature that denied to you, Edumenio, and to you, Henrietta, the gift of happiness that God had bestowed upon you.

Literature interprets existence, and in so doing, it not only provides understanding but also touches emotional chords. Some of the prevalent themes of recent Hispanic writers include dislocation and migration, social exploitation by the Anglo, barrio life, and struggle for self-definition. They also experiment with the language, using both English and Spanish.

Just as some Native Americans, many Hispanic writers see the mechanical and technological as sinister. The poet links it with exploitation and alienation. Technology's development is an improved method of killing people in vast numbers. It is knowledge without the wisdom of nature. Anaya alludes to it briefly in *Bless Me, Ultima*, treating it as hubris:

> I heard many grown-ups blame the harsh winter and the sandstorms of spring on the new bomb that had been made to end the war. "The atomic bomb," they whispered, "a ball of white heat beyond the imagination, beyond hell—And they pointed south, beyond the green valley of El Puerto. "Man was not made to know so

much," the old ladies cried in hushed, hoarse voices,
"they compete with God, they disturb the seasons, they
seek to know more than God Himself. In the end, that
knowledge they seek will destroy us all. . . . "

The future of literature written by Hispanics looks optimistic.
New voices are raised, new explanations of reality. It clearly
reflects the vital forces of a people's inner dimension, be they
passions, sufferings, or simply flashes of their circumstances.

The group we label as "Anglo" is really made up of a variety
of ethnic and racial backgrounds—English, Irish, German,
Polish, and so on. But for the most part, the majority of these
people have been absorbed into the mainstream of American
ideology, embracing wholeheartedly the ideals of assimilation,
individual achievement, and self-definition. Many did not
preserve or do not emphasize the distinct language, religious
practices, cultural traits, or distinct traditions of their heritage.
In New Mexico, they are viewed simply as White Americans.

New Mexico saw no significant Anglo influx until the
beginning of the nineteenth century, when trappers and traders
first trickled through the northern mountains. These mountain
men and wandering peddlers posed no immediate threat to
what had been for more than two hundred years a bicultural
state. The opening of the Santa Fe Trail in 1821, however,
signaled the beginning of an intrusion that would change it
forever. By 1846, when General Stephen Kearny's troops con-
quered New Mexico, there were Anglo traders, trappers, farmers, housewives, and children living here.

Keith Wilson's poem "The New Mexican" captures the
flavor of these early mountain men:

> Old mountain men, born
> and raised for the power of their hands, and arms
> —valuing themselves little past those physical

strengths—and what survival finally cost them
when necessities, time, disappeared
with the game. . . .

Harvey Fergusson's novels provide a literary perspective of this era because he generally sets his stories in the past. Each of his novels is grounded in an impressive layer of detail. *In Those Days* (1936), for example, is based in part on the real-life exploits of Fergusson's grandfather, Franz Huning, who was one of the early traders on the Santa Fe Trail. Kevin McIlvoy's short story "The Complete History of New Mexico," on the other hand, is a humorous spoof of the development of New Mexico written in thirteen pages. Full of vague generalities, incorrect assumptions, and false chronicles, McIlvoy's story satirizes the history texts that have also minimized or left out large portions of New Mexico's historical experience.

Another, primarily Texan, influence swept into New Mexico after the Civil War. The green valleys of the western half of the state and the high plains on the east side were soon enveloped by herds of cattle competing with the native sheep of the Hispanic population. In the last quarter of the nineteenth century, prospectors and miners began to populate isolated niches in the state.

Businesses in New Mexico had been small in scale, limited to individual tradesmen and peddlers prior to 1846, but the change in government also saw a revolution in business practices. A new kind of merchant, one who had received his training in the mercantile centers of Europe or along the East Coast, came to Las Vegas, Santa Fe, Bernalillo, and other towns, and not only presented customers with a wider selection of goods, but extended credit, built up inventories, and changed the face of many small towns.

The coming of the railroads in the 1870s played a significant role in the importation of many new ideas, cultures, and people to New Mexico. The railroads linked remote parts of the state and solidified mining and cattle enterprises; provided transportation for people, goods, and cattle; and brought to the railroad towns solid midwestern folks. The newcomers brought with them new ideas about architecture, opinions on public schooling and government, and a wide range of backgrounds, surnames, and traditions.

By the beginning of the twentieth century, whole sections of central and eastern New Mexico were dominated by Anglo populations. The arrival of tubercular patients—for whom large hospitals, nursing homes, and sanatoriums were built in Albuquerque, Las Vegas, and other towns—assured the emergence of a new majority. To this mixture of citizens were added the soldiers and scientists of the 1940s and 1950s in places like Alamogordo, Clovis, Albuquerque, and the new town of Los Alamos. Service industries followed, and universities and school systems developed and grew to serve the burgeoning population. Later, a new kind of refugee began to arrive. Retirees moved to New Mexico where housing was reasonable and winters warm. Hippies, living in tepees, garishly painted buses, and geodesic domes, peopled remote valleys around Taos.

The early writings of the Anglo-American settlers naturally belong to the tradition of the Virginia and New England colonists. In 1625, Samuel Purchas, in his famous *Pilgrimages*, gave to the English-reading public a brief but rather accurate account of Friar Marcos; Esteban, a black Moorish slave; and Coronado's search for the fabled cities of gold. Writing with more sense of participation began when a succession of men and women came to the early Southwest not on a visit but to be part of the life about which they wrote. James O. Pattie, George Kendall, Susan Shelby Magoffin, Josiah Gregg, Lewis Garrard, and Kit Carson wrote factual narratives of their experiences.

A large proportion of twentieth-century fiction based in
New Mexico brings the Anglo and Spanish cultures into contact, contrast, and often conflict. Of the novels relating to
contacts between Hispanics and Anglos, Harvey Fergusson's
Grant of Kingdom (1950) is a classic. It begins as the story of an
omnipotent Taos trapper and mountaineer, Jean Ballard. The
hero, closely patterned after Lucien Beaubien Maxwell, meets
and is captivated by the daughter of a Spanish patron of Taos,
marries her, and receives as dowry a huge, undeveloped tract of
land identifiable as the Maxwell Land Grant. Ballard's generos-
ity toward Hispanic and Texan alike, and his overextension in
all directions, lead to his eventual loss of the land. The novel,
however, treats the conflicts and accommodation between
Hispanics and Anglos that has been the subject of a consider-
able volume of literature.

Far less muted are the conflicts related in a number of other
novels. The antagonisms between Anglo and Hispanic are
relatively innocent, if intense, in Richard Bradford's *Red Sky at
Morning* (1968), which tells of an adolescent's awakening in a
small town, a caricature of Santa Fe. The story is usually
humorous, usually believable, and sympathetic to each of the
groups portrayed.

Crosswinds (1987) by Michael Thomas, although predominantly about the hypocrisy of modern society, which destroys
the uniqueness inherent in rural communities, also deals with
Hispanic-Anglo encounters. Rodney, the main character, finds
a job on an all-Mexican building crew. They accept him without
prejudice, and Rodney considers what the result would be if the
situation were reversed:

> The guys on the crew were less tense with each other
> than white fellows usually are. On most jobs white guys
> are always a bit on edge about who knows most and who

makes small decisions too trivial for the foreman. This
crew didn't seem to care. . . . I wondered how well a
Mexican would be treated on an all white man crew. I
didn't have to wonder too much.

New Mexico is also a western state, heir to cowboy legends
and country drawls. As such, it has produced several writers
who brought talent and knowledge to books of the "Western"
class. Eugene Manlove Rhodes, who rode the range along the
Jornada del Muerto, later turned his experiences into a great
many short stories and several novels. The cowboy of the past
is still in the saddle in much of the art and literature. The men
are strong and violent, and vengeance is a dominant theme.
Whether as sheriff or outlaw, he performs the same cultural
function: he brings in his wake the modern world. Billy the Kid,
a figure of international renown, undoubtedly stands as the
best-known New Mexican in history. And Kid mania continues. Two Pulitzer Prize-winning authors have tackled Billy:
first, Larry McMurtry, in 1988, with *Anything for Billy*; and
then N. Scott Momaday, in 1989, with *The Ancient Child.*
Momaday's Billy is handsome, daring, and articulate. "It has
something to do with legend," Momaday writes, "and with the
way we must think of ourselves, we cowboys and Indians, we
roughriders of the world. We are lovers of violence, aren't we?"
  Many writers were inspired by the land, history, and people
in the state. Many even wrote about common events or things.
Gene Frumkin, for example, wrote a poem on Indian corn:

> Indian corn suspended from the ceiling
> eight stalks wired together One is yellow
> one maroon another pink still another black
> These colors are imprecise they harmonize
> with, and are, the language that observes them

hanging, at this angle, just above
the horizontal window This angle
is the eye's
      Another corn is creamy
three others have no words The numbering
is exact, the sizes of corn descend
from smallest to largest
with two exceptions; again, there is definition
in the numbering
      These cornstalks have been hanging
around for more than two years, the exact date
of their acquisition lost
though the place, Acoma Pueblo, remains
They instill no ideas
no fantasies The mind, holding them, is static
itself suspended; the hand has no impulse
to covet their polished surface What is of concern
is that, at last, they are visible

And Patricia Clark Smith writes about the rituals associated
with Good Friday, in her poem "San Luis, New Mexico":

At San Luis, on Good Friday,
they reenact the crucifixion.
¿Cómo los penitentes?
–No, señora, nada de sangre,
no blood, a light cross.
Three hundred yards from church to chapel,
small crosses like children make for pets' graves
to mark each station.
The Christ is twelve, with a speech defect;
. . . and the Mary who is no better than she should be,
dressed in whorehouse black, lovely twelve year old limbs
comes on to lift the boy man she loves
with a world awakening on her face

The real fact of Los Alamos, Alamogordo, and the Manhattan Project, which propelled the entire world into the Atomic Age, has an impact on many writers. Edith Warner, a former teacher, rented a dilapidated house at Otowi Bridge. With a talent for creating beauty, she turned the ugly house into a haven for nearby Pueblo natives and Anglo scientists alike. She is the subject of fiction, in Frank Waters's *The Woman at Otowi Crossing* (1966), and of documentary, in Peggy Pond Church's *The House at Otowi Bridge* (1959). In both, the disparate worlds of San Ildefonso pueblo and Los Alamos's wartime Manhattan Project meet. John Nichols, on the other hand, talks about the problem of making a film about nuclear physics in the twentieth century, about waiting for the nuclear holocaust. He says the problem is "how to get the human imagination to imagine something that is basically so horrible it's unimaginable. To imagine it in a vivid enough way that people will be moved and will put energy into trying to avoid it. If you make it too palatable or too diverting, too artistic, people can ignore it. If you make it too horrible, they can't watch it."

Grubb Graebner's play, *Winners of the White Atomic Sweepstakes* (1984) emphasizes modern doubt and anxiety resulting from our technological abilities. In this mostly humorous play, two friends are trying to avoid cynicism and despair by linking physics with Native American mysticism.

> LARRY: Black holes become exits into paradise, unified
>   fields become proof that we're all parts of the
>   cosmic corn dance.
> STACY: Sorry I asked.
> LARRY: It always amuses me when religion looks for
>   certitude in a science built on doubt.
> STACY: Fred isn't religious.
> LARRY: So these are Fred's ideas.

STACY: He just has an appreciation for the Indian way
of thinking.

Contemporary artists and writers remain captivated by the
landscape's bold beauty and mystery. Keith Wilson, in "Valley
of the Rio Chama," writes:

> Most of us here today are artists of some sort, all caught
> embarrassed before this magnificence, these glories of
> canyons, bluffs carved into standing hooded figures,
> multicolored giant crayons the sun has melted until they
> stand layer upon layer in rich pastels, as if a prism had
> broken strewing raw light into colors, freezing them
> there in sand stone clay.

But the writing now is also beginning to be shaped by the
state's modern mix of gaudy pretensions, glib, get-rich aspira-
tions, and the somber struggles to find a sane and secure place
amid the whirl of change. Writers are seeking a coherent vision
arising out of a love for those realities that can be reached,
asserted, celebrated. Some rely on impersonal forms, others on a
more intimate language of experience even with a sense of irony,
perhaps in order to come to terms with the possibility of destroying
so much around us and to fight against the complacency.

Besides the larger three ethnic groups, other ethnic cultures also add to the diversity and richness that is New Mexico
and contribute to the mosaic. African-Americans, for example,
slowly trickled into New Mexico. With the Emancipation Pro-
clamation and the end of the Civil War, freed slaves sought
refuge in many states and territories across the Mason-Dixon
line. New Mexico became a haven for many. Most cowboys who
came west as slaves were roping and branding before they became free men. One of the early cowboys to come to New

Mexico was Nigger Frank, who rode for John Chisum. One of the most respected cowboys was Nigger Add Jones, range boss of the LFD Ranch in Otero County. However, it is sad that although Black cowboys had ridden through the real West, they found no place in the West of fiction.

On July 28, 1866, Congress passed an act that provided for six Black regiments in the regular U.S. Army. The Black troops were called less than complimentary names by white troops. However, when the Indians named them "Buffalo Soldiers," it was accepted and recognized as an indication of the Indians' respect. There were many notable men among the Buffalo Soldiers. One of these men was Lt. Henry Ossian Flipper, the first Black man to graduate from West Point. After service, he spent thirty-seven years as a civil engineer in Mexico and New Mexico. He helped draw the boundaries of New Mexico.

After the death of slavery, the belief in Black inferiority remained. Black migrants found they had not run from traditional American attitudes; they followed them into New Mexico. Here, they faced segregated communities, schools, beatings, and threats. One of the major injustices shown toward the Black person in New Mexico is to ignore his presence in the state and his many contributions. African-Americans are excluded as being a culture in the overall makeup of the state; but they did participate in events in New Mexico and were very much in evidence. Some of the important African-Americans from New Mexico included Dr. Ralph Bunche, United Nations troubleshooter and winner of the Nobel Peace Prize, and John Lewis, international composer and musician of modern jazz. They are not included in most textbooks, which is a sad, regrettable oversight.

African-American artists and writers in modern New Mexico are beginning to make their experience recognized. Larry Heard's photography, for example, uses technology and media to show the distorted, disjointed view we often have of the world. Jo Ann Harper combines symbols of African-American, Native American, and Australian Aborigine life in the creation of her painted gourds and masks. Peggi Randolf takes a lighthearted look at being Black in America. Other artists, such as Carl Peniston, Willie Blecher, and Marie Holmes, believe that being Black has little or no part in their art. Maisha Baton, a poet, short-story writer, and playwright, says that her speaking and writing grew out of an interest in her heritage as a Black woman. She began writing plays about the history of Blacks in this region. Her most recent play, "Kate's Sister," uses Kate Williams, an expert sharpshooter and horseback rider, as a starting point. Another of Baton's plays, "Mitote," tells the story of Black women in New Mexico from the viewpoints of three women sitting on a front porch. The weaving of cultures is evident in the title.

Another group with an interesting history in our state are the Japanese. There are about twelve hundred persons of Japanese ancestry living in the state. Like other children of immigrants, Japanese-Americans in New Mexico grew up enveloped in American culture, giving little thought to their heritage. In the 1970s, however, many Japanese in New Mexico began to be fascinated by their own family and ethnic histories. There was a growing interest in traditional Japanese food, martial arts, and Japanese arts such as ikebana flower arranging and bonsai techniques of growing plants that seem to contain entire landscapes in a single pot. The celebration of Omatsuri is now held once a year, featuring Japanese food, dance, art, and history.

The Japanese population in New Mexico was very small and generally drawn here by the coal-mining industry. However, when the Japanese bombed Pearl Harbor, the number of Japanese-Americans in New Mexico grew dramatically. The sudden growth occurred almost overnight—and almost entirely in secret. Japanese, all of them men, were imprisoned in two New Mexico detention camps run by the Department of Justice. One of the camps, on the outskirts of Santa Fe, held up to twenty-one hundred internees. Few of those kept in the camps here remained in New Mexico after the war.

New Mexican Japanese, too, have contributed in numerous ways to the culture and history of the state. Ruth Hashimoto, for example, was instrumental in bringing the Sister Cities program to the state when Sasebo and Albuquerque became sister cities in 1966. The late Roy Nakayama, agriculture scientist at New Mexico State University, was nicknamed "Mr. Chile" for developing several strains of chile that have helped to make chile New Mexico's number one cash crop.

Other ethnic groups, including Jews, Chinese, and, recently, Vietnamese, are a very small minority in the state, but all of them provide an angle from which to view modern New Mexico, and each changes the view.

A variety of views comprise the literature of New Mexico. Writers from each of the cultural groups write from their particular perspective. Slowly, the contemporary writings of the Hispanic and Native American communities are beginning to make an impact on the region. But ethnic groups, too, cannot bury their proverbial heads and succumb to uncritical glorification of ethnicity. The ethnic impulse necessarily carries with it dangers of parochialism. But the ethnic sanctuary is not enough; it must be transcended, especially at a time when the fate of humankind is increasingly an international fate.

It is imperative to be aware and accepting of the differences among the various ethnic groups that meet in New Mexico. It is equally important to look beneath the surface to see the unifying forces, the traits common to the whole. Writers and artists have noted the prevalence of sun and wind and blue skies; the persisting frontier; the tenacity with which the many ethnic groups prevail. But the lives of all New Mexicans are coterminous with those of the society as a whole. New Mexicans can generally see twenty-five, sometimes one hundred, miles to the horizon. Hopefully, that farsightedness can also extend to a vision of holistic humanity and humaneness even while preserving our distinctive ethnic identity.

BIBLIOGRAPHY

Listed here are those books and articles most important and valuable to understanding this subject. The list is not meant to be exhaustive.

Several bibliographical collections are available, particularly on Anglo art, artists, and writers, but the sources listed below primarily list Hispanic and Native American work, which is less easily accessible. Francisco A. Lomelí and Donaldo W. Urioste, *Chicano Perspectives in Literature: A Critical and Annotated Bibliography* (Albuquerque: Pajarito Publications, 1976), is written strictly from a literary perspective. It includes critical evaluations on the importance and impact of Chicano literature. F. Arturo Rosales and David William Foster, *Hispanics and the Humanities in the Southwest: A Directory of Resources* (Arizona: Center for Latin American Studies, 1983), includes a useful chapter on New Mexico by E. A. Mares. Roberto G. Trujillo and Andres Rodríguez, eds., *Literature Chicana: Creative and Critical Writings through 1984* (Oakland, Calif.: Floricanto Press, 1985), is an excellent bibliography; while Tom Lewis, *Storied New Mexico: An Annotated Bibliography of Novels with New Mexico Settings* (Albuquerque: University of New Mexico Press, 1991), includes works written by New Mexican as well as non-New Mexican authors.

Francisco Jiménez, ed., *The Identification and Analysis of Chicano Literature* (New York: Bilingual Press, 1979), makes available a number of important and useful published and unpublished critical essays on Chicano literature and provides background and critical trends in this field. Erlinda Gonzales-Berry, ed., *Pasó por Aquí: Critical Essays on New Mexico Literary Tradition, 1542–1988*

(Albuquerque: University of New Mexico Press, 1989), is an excellent source for Hispanics in literature, whereas Charles L. Briggs, *Competence in Performance: The Creativity of Tradition in Mexicano Verbal Art* (Philadelphia: University of Pennsylvania Press, 1988), contains important material on folklore as well as on customs and social life in New Mexico.

Other excellent collections furnish a variety of literary works. Rudolfo A. Anaya has been the most influential and prolific Hispanic promoter of literature by New Mexicans, and several of the anthologies he has edited include a variety of short fiction and poetry by writers of many ethnic groups in New Mexico. For example, see Rudolfo A. Anaya and Antonio Márquez, eds., *Cuentos Chicanos* (Albuquerque: New America, UNM, 1980); Anaya, ed., *Voces: An Anthology of Nuevo Mexicano Writers* (Albuquerque: University of New Mexico Press, 1980); Anaya, ed., *Tierra: Contemporary Short Fiction of New Mexico* (El Paso: Cinco Puntos Press, 1989); and Anaya and Antonio Márquez, eds., *Cuentos Chicanos: A Short Anthology* (Albuquerque: New America, 1988). An annual anthology begun in 1989 by the English Department at the University of New Mexico also includes many new as well as established contemporary writers: Anaya, ed., *Blue Mesa Review* (Albuquerque: Creative Writing Center, UNM, 1989).

Although another anthology focuses on writings by Native Americans, Black, Chicana, and Asian-American women from throughout the United States, it likewise includes short fiction and poetry by New Mexico writers: Dexter Fisher, ed., *The Third Woman: Minority Women Writers of the United States* (Boston: Houghton Mifflin, 1980). An excellent source for writing by Hispanic New Mexican women writers is Tey Diana Rebolledo, Erlinda Gonzales-Berry, and Teresa Márquez, eds., *Las Mujeres Hablan: An Anthology of Nuevo Mexicana Writers* (Albuquerque: El Norte Publications, 1988). Joan M. Jensen and Darlis A. Miller, eds., *New Mexico Women: Intercultural Perspectives* (Albuquerque: University of New Mexico Press, 1986), also contains excellent essays that give a historical understanding of the lives of women in New Mexico from 1535 to 1960. In addition, Paula Gunn Allen, ed., *Spider Woman's Granddaughters* (New York: Fawcett Columbine, 1989), furnishes an excellent resource for Native American women writers, including Misha Gallagher and Soge Track.

Besides anthologies, specific ethnic novels and collections of short fiction, drama, and poetry are noteworthy. Some of the most popular and, perhaps, significant, because of their impact on New Mexico culture and literary history, include the following: Rudolfo A. Anaya, *Bless Me, Ultima* (Berkeley: Quinto Sol, 1972); Anaya, *Heart of Aztlan* (Berkeley: Justa Publications, 1976); Anaya, *Alburquerque* (Albuquerque: University of New Mexico Press, 1992); Denise Chavez, *The Last of the Menu Girls* (Houston: Arte Publico Press, 1986); Sabine R. Ulibarrí, *Tierra Amarilla: Stories of New Mexico* (Albuquerque: University of New Mexico Press, 1971); Paula Gunn Allen, *The Woman Who Owned the Shadows* (San Francisco: Spinsters/ Aunt Lute, 1983); Leslie Marmon Silko, *Ceremony* (New York: Viking, 1977); and Silko, *Almanac of the Dead* (New York: Simon and Schuster, 1991); the many detective novels of Tony Hillerman, including *The Blessing Way* (New York: Harper Collins, 1970); Michael A. Thomas, *Crosswinds* (Albuquerque: Amador Publishers, 1987); and V. B. Price and Kirk Gittings, *Chaco Body* (Albuquerque: Artspace Press, 1991).

A useful book on Native American education and, thereby, significant to an understanding of a people's way of life, is Sally Hyer, *One House, One Voice, One Heart: Native American Education at the Santa Fe Indian School* (Santa Fe: Museum of New Mexico Press, 1990). A good overview is Joe S. Sando, *The Pueblo Indians* (San Francisco: Indian Historian Press, 1979). Alfonso Ortiz, ed., *New Perspectives on the Pueblos* (Albuquerque: University of New Mexico Press, 1972), collects essays on Pueblo Indians of Arizona and New Mexico and includes sections on ritual drama, mythology, and music. Although primarily a collection of the women's writings on nature, Lorraine Anderson, ed., *Sisters of the Earth: Women's Prose and Poetry about Nature* (New York: Vintage, 1991), contains works by Luci Tapahonso, Leslie Marmon Silko, and Paula Gunn Allen.

Useful perspectives on New Mexico, primarily from Anglo viewpoints, include John F. Crawford, William Balassi, and Annie O. Eysturoy, eds., *This Is About Vision: Interviews with Southwestern*

Writers (Albuquerque: University of New Mexico Press, 1990), a notable collection that contains conversations with Frank Waters, John Nichols, Mark Medoff, Pat Mora, Jimmy Santiago Baca, and Luci Tapahonso. A valuable source for contemporary drama is David Richard Jones, ed., *New Mexico Plays* (Albuquerque: University of New Mexico Press, 1989). An overview volume on contemporary western history with an excellent chapter on culture, including literature and art, is Michael P. Malone and Richard W. Etulain, *The American West* (Lincoln: University of Nebraska Press, 1989). Also, see Mabel Major and T. M. Pearce, *Southwest Heritage: A Literary History with Bibliography*, 3d ed. (Albuquerque: University of New Mexico Press, 1972).

Meanwhile, Russell Martin and Marc Barasch, eds., *Writers of the Purple Sage: An Anthology of Recent Western Writing* (New York: Penguin, 1984), rather than selecting western stories in the Zane Grey and John Wayne tradition, focus on contemporary writers and their views of the modern West. William T. Pilkington, *My Blood's Country: Studies in Southwestern Literature* (Fort Worth: Texas Christian University Press, 1973), is a collection of essays, while Cordelia Candelaria, ed., *Multiethnic Literature of the United States: Critical Introductions and Classroom Resources* (Boulder: University of Colorado, 1989), is especially useful for teachers. A. LaVonne Brown Ruoff and Jerry W. Ward, Jr., *Redefining American Literary History* (New York: Modern Language Association of America, 1990), discusses the canon in American literature and the role of ethnic groups in literature.

Material culture also supplies important information on ethnic experiences in New Mexico. Most museums house artifacts that illuminate the lives of ethnic peoples. Moreover, numerous art galleries throughout the state are also important sources of information not only for the creative efforts of our artists, but also for the changing perspectives they furnish of our multiethnic state.

SIX

THE CULTURES OF MODERN NEW MEXICO, 1940-1990

FERENC M. SZASZ

NEW Mexico is a unique land. Both long-time residents and first-time visitors agree on that. But exactly where does the uniqueness lie? Here there is no agreement. The most common interpretation has been that of the "Three Cultures." It is the presence of the Native American, Hispanic, and "Anglo-Pioneer" cultures, this argument goes, that accounts for New Mexico's distinctive qualities. Albuquerque writer Erna Fergusson voiced this eloquently in her *New Mexico: A Pageant of Three Peoples* (1951), as did Roswell native Paul Horgan in *The Heroic Triad* (1965). The annual Taos fiesta nicely reflects this theme by selecting *three* queens, one from each ethnic group.

Historians have spilled a good deal of ink discussing exactly how these cultures have interacted with each other over time. Many an early twentieth-century study suggested that all three blended in easy harmony. Fergusson and Horgan both emphasized their relatively peaceful coexistence. But a 1993 analysis is a bit more cautious, suggesting that "although the three cultures intermingle, they never completely blend."

The "Three Cultures" approach to New Mexico has become virtual orthodoxy. Historians have come up with no other frame of analysis. For someone to argue that the half-century since World War II has altered the "three-culture" equation is tantamount to heresy. It might compare with questioning the centrality of Scripture in the *Southern Baptist Newsletter*. But historians rush in where angels fear to tread, and I plan to do precisely that. The thesis of this essay is both simple and complex: during the past half-century, New Mexicans have had to confront several new "cultures." In turn, these cultures have fostered, overlapped, blended with, and, at times, transformed the "heroic triad" of New Mexico's ancient past.

The first new "culture" is the culture of landscape. From the frying-pan flatness of the Llano Estacado to the alpine beauty of the northern mountains, New Mexico's landforms have ever inflamed the imagination. Modern scientists have counted six of the seven climate zones in the state, from the Lower Sonoran along the southern border to the Arctic-Alpine atop Wheeler Peak. The Bisti Badlands, south of Farmington, have achieved international fame as the best fossil bed on the globe to study the end of the Cretaceous Period. The land of New Mexico has always been a source of wonder.

While the landforms themselves have changed little since the 1930s, the landscape itself has altered considerably. After the war, the federal government withdrew millions of acres to create military bases and missile ranges at Clovis, Albuquerque, Alamogordo, and Roswell. Increased regulations by the National Forest Service, National Park Service, Bureau of Land Management, and various state agencies became a fact of life. Simultaneously, as easy access to public lands diminished, the state population increased steadily.

The statistics tell a relentless tale. From a small town of about 45,000 in 1942, Albuquerque mushroomed into a sprawling metropolis of over 380,000 in 1990. During the 1980s, the Las Cruces area was hailed as one of the fastest growing regions of the nation. The overall state population increased accordingly:

1940:	531,818
1950:	681,187
1960:	951.023
1970:	1,017,055
1980:	1,303,393
1990:	1,515,069

Faced with such pressures, all levels of government found themselves "managing" the natural resources via increasingly complex rules and regulations. Consider the role of the state Department of Game and Fish as an example. Although concern over the fate of local trout, bear, beaver, elk, and deer reached back to the early years of the century, wildlife-management programs increased steadily after the Second World War. In the late 1940s, for example, the department released a herd of Bighorn sheep into the Sandia Mountains to replenish the original stock; a few years later they repeated the process with Barbary sheep in the Guadalupe Mountains. In the 1960s, they set loose yet more Bighorn into the Pecos Wilderness. From the 1950s to the 1970s, the Department of Game and Fish also released such exotic animals as Aoudad sheep, kudu, Siberian ibex, and Siberian gemsboks (oryx) into the New Mexican terrain. In the 1980s, officials laid plans to reintroduce the Mexican wolf (Lobo) and the mountain lion—both of which drew heated protests from state ranchers and sheepmen.

With few exceptions these programs of wildlife reintroductions have met with only modest success. The state abandoned its pheasant and prairie chicken release program in the 1950s, and actually had to recapture and treat some disease-plagued Barbary sheep in the Guadalupes. In the late 1970s, public opinion so turned against the introduction of exotic species that the entire project was shelved. Only the successful fish-hatchery program has escaped criticism.

Although most New Mexicans admit that some variety of land and wildlife management is necessary, there is little agreement on details. Virtually every issue—from banding mountain lions with radio collars to "thinning" the feral burro herd at Bandelier National Monument—brings forth heated argument. Some programs, such as the 1990 fitting of Jornada Angora goats with radioactive collars to determine which coyote ate which goat (the "Atomic Goat" project) have been complete fiascoes. Perhaps the situation was best illustrated in a 1986 near-fatal bear attack on a Philmont Ranch Boy Scout camper. A Santa Fe spokesman saw this incident as a metaphor for the state's dilemma: "Everybody is running out of room."

Few artists have captured the beauty of the New Mexican landscape better than the region's photographers. In fact, New Mexico has attracted more famous photographers than any other state except, perhaps, California. Much of this attraction may be traced to, in the words of author Charles F. Lummis, "that ineffable clarity, that luminousness, which makes a photographic light to be matched in no other civilized country."

During the 1940s, the state's most well-known photographers, John Candelario, Ernest Knee, and Laura Gilpin, all lived in the vicinity of Santa Fe. Gilpin's classic portrayal of Native peoples in *The Pueblos: A Camera Chronicle* (1941) and *The Enduring Navajo* (1968) were each the product of over a decade of effort. Her *Rio Grande: River of Destiny* (1949) portrayed in black and white photographs what Paul Horgan's *The Great River* (1954) conveyed in words.

The Fine Arts section of the University of New Mexico gave local photography a boost when it introduced new majors in the discipline during the early 1960s. Professor Van Deren

New Mexico's distinct religious tradition is captured in John S. Candelario's Two Crosses. *(Courtesy University Art Museum, University of New Mexico, neg. no. 81.29)*

Coke brought in talented professional photographers, such as Anne Noggle and Betty Hahn, and, especially, art historian Beaumont Newhall. Widely acknowledged as the "founder" of the history of photography, Newhall attracted a large number of graduate students to the field. Albuquerque galleries, such as White Oak, Quivira, and the University Art Museum, plus Camera West and the Andrew Smith Gallery in Santa Fe, provided the public with opportunities to view photographic images. The first New Mexico Photographers Exhibition was not staged until 1956, but within twelve years a New York City art judge declared the state's photography of "very high calibre—as good as anything in the country." The photographs of Todd Webb, Meridel Rubenstein, Paul Caponigro, and Patrick Nagatani, plus the publishing emphasis of the University of New Mexico Press, have kept the town of Santa Fe, and much of the state, "synonymous with photography over the years."

Two of America's most famous contemporary photographers, Ansel Adams and Eliot Porter, both have strong New Mexico links. Born in California and trained as a classical musician, Adams fell in love with the state on his first visit to Taos and returned to photograph thousands of New Mexican scenes. In fact, Adams's most widely known photograph is his black-and-white rendition of *Moonrise, Hernandez, New Mexico*, which he shot one late afternoon in 1941. For nearly fifty years, this brooding, majestic village scene has stood as testimony both to the mystery of New Mexico as well as to the vision of the photographer. Yet as Adams confessed in 1974, *Moonrise* owed as much to his darkroom skills as to the placement of his camera. The actual sky was not so dark, he admitted, nor did the crosses in the cemetery shine quite so brightly. *Moonrise* thus became "a distortion, but not a distortion." "Reality was not that way at all," Adams admitted. "But it felt that way."

Even more famous than Ansel Adams was longtime Tesuque resident, Eliot Porter. Born in Illinois, Porter, like Adams, came to photography via another discipline, having first trained as a physician and taught biochemistry at Harvard until 1939. That year, art impresario Alfred Stieglitz gave Porter his first show— twenty-nine black-and-white images—at Stieglitz's famous gallery, An American Place, in New York City. Afterward, Porter resigned his teaching job to devote the rest of his life to photography. Although he began with large-scale landscapes, he soon turned to depicting the more intimate details of nature, almost a "miniaturization" of the world around him. "Only in fragments of the whole is nature's order apparent," Porter wrote in 1990.

Moving to New Mexico permanently in 1946, Porter proceeded to master the difficult art of the dye transfer color printing process. In fact, his ability to manipulate color in the darkroom soon elevated the dye transfer procedure to a genuine art form. Porter's first book, *In Wildness Is the Preservation of the World* (1962), helped to establish the Sierra Club's reputation, as well as his own. Two dozen books followed, including his classic *Birds of North America* (1972) and *Eliot Porter's Southwest* (1985). Often termed "the Ansel Adams of color photography"—a designation he disliked—Eliot Porter reigned as the world's foremost nature photographer until his death in the fall of 1990.

When purists accused Eliot Porter of distorting nature by manipulating her colors in the dye transfer process, he would reply that the colors were already there. All he did was simply enhance or diminish them.Porter felt free to alter the colors because the essential quality of a photograph rested not with its "literalism" but with the "emotional impact" that it had on the viewer.

It may seem a bit of a leap from trout hatcheries and newly released Bighorn sheep to the darkrooms of Ansel Adams and Eliot Porter. But perhaps the gap is not so wide after all. Whether one confronts New Mexico's landscape directly, in the Jemez Mountains or Pecos Wilderness, or indirectly via the imagery of Adams and Porter, the results are similar. In both cases, one interacts with *managed* landscape. Increased control of land and landscape has become a central aspect of New Mexican life since 1942. The wild regions of the prewar years have virtually disappeared.

Second is the culture of "big science." Although New Mexico hosted its share of astronomers, physicians, and anthropologists before World War II, big science began in earnest in the fall of 1942. That year the U.S. Army informed the headmaster of the Los Alamos Ranch School that their facilities were needed for the national war effort. Construction began immediately, and officials predicted that the proposed town of Los Alamos would eventually house perhaps two hundred scientists and their families. By 1945, however, the population reached seven thousand and showed no signs of slowing. As the most crucial cog in the sprawling Anglo-American Manhattan Project, the Los Alamos scientists wrestled with a momentous assignment: to produce an atomic weapon to end World War II "in the shortest possible time."

The atomic age began at 5:30 A.M., July 16, 1945, at the strangely named "Trinity Site," about thirty-five miles east of Socorro. The location, now part of the White Sands Missile Range, still appears on most maps. From that moment forward, New Mexico would forever be termed "the birthplace of the atomic age." Local residents knew of the existence of a mammoth bomb in July; the world learned of atomic weapons three weeks later at Hiroshima and Nagasaki. Within days, Los Alamos had achieved a worldwide reputation, the first New Mexican city to do so.

The town of Los Alamos also introduced the state to massive federal funding for scientific purposes. But would it continue in time of peace? After V-J Day, many officials expressed doubts that Los Alamos would survive. As the famed "first team" of scientists departed for their peacetime university jobs, pundits predicted that Los Alamos would join Shakespeare or Mogollon as simply an unique variety of New Mexico ghost town.

General Leslie R. Groves, the overall head of the Manhattan Project, argued vigorously for making Los Alamos permanent. He noted that the nation would never again be able to rebuild such a community. Norris Bradbury, who took over as director of the laboratory from famed scientist J. Robert Oppenheimer, felt the same way. In mid-1946, Bradbury issued his famous "go or stay" directive to wavering scientists and technical personnel. He also supervised the transition from secret wartime military base to New Mexico's first "federal city."

From 1942 to the mid-1950s, Los Alamos formed a completely federal town. The government owned everything—houses, laboratories, shops, and all else. One needed a pass to enter the gate. Of equal importance, in an isolated section of a very poor state, the government paid high wages.

The impact of these wages soon spread beyond the town itself to affect the entire region. Contractors, carpenters, electricians, truck drivers, merchants, restauranteurs, barbers, artists, grocers, farmers, and maids all benefited accordingly. Historian Chris Dietz has argued that the nearby Tewa-speaking pueblos of San Ildefonso, Santa Clara, and Cochiti used Los Alamos salaries to *preserve* their historic Native traditions. Pueblo leaders were able to purchase communal farm equipment, and numerous other Indians followed suit on an individual basis. A town of cultured, highly educated outsiders also provided a new outlet for Native arts and crafts. The same impact may be seen in the nearby Hispanic villages. Cordova wood carver George Lopez supported his family, in part, by working at Los Alamos; in his spare time he revived, almost singlehandedly, an historic Hispanic craft. The nearby, predominantly Hispanic community of Española also sent its sons and daughters to work at Los Alamos. It might not be too much to suggest that a legacy of big science (or, perhaps, big technology) also found its way into the colorful, if somewhat perplexing, art of the sophisticated hydraulic lifts that adorn the Española low riders. (The city proudly claims to be "the low rider capital of the nation.") By the mid-1980s, Los Alamos National Laboratories employed over seven thousand people and had a budget of half a billion dollars. Such a presence permanently altered the economy of northern New Mexico.

The culture of science reached into other areas of the state as well. Historian Necah Stewart Furman has shown how the establishment of Sandia National Laboratories in Albuquerque altered life in the Duke City. Like Los Alamos, Sandia brought in thousands of highly educated, sophisticated outsiders. In addition, it employed people from all ranks of life: technicians, security guards, secretaries, teachers, file clerks, and others. By the mid-1960s, Sandia employed over eight thousand people. The rise of Kirtland Air Force Base, especially the closely related Special Weapons Laboratory, funneled even more federal monies into Bernalillo County. Although "Sandia" is not a widely recognized name outside of New Mexico, the mass production of nuclear weapons that occurred there from the 1950s forward made it indispensable to the national defense system.

The name of Paddy Martinez is well known to all residents of Grants and Milan, for in the early 1950s the Navajo sheep-herder discovered a chunk of uranium that inaugurated the biggest American mining boom since the California Gold Rush of 1849. Known previously as a spot to raise fine carrots, by the mid-1960s Grants basked in the reputation of the "Uranium Capital of the United States." By 1980 over 40 percent of the nation's uranium was mined and milled in the Grants Uranium Belt region, and the town reached a population of 11,500. Forecasters predicted a population of 100,000 by the year 2000 and jested that Albuquerque would simply become a suburb of Grants. Although private corporations financed the mining operations, federal weapons demands lay behind this boom that transformed all of west-central New Mexico.

The Tularosa Basin underwent similar scientific transformation. Although New Mexico writer Ross Calvin once urged that the entire basin be set aside as a permanent outdoor natural laboratory, such was not to be. In the 1930s, Massachusetts scientist Robert Goddard chose nearby Roswell to test his rocket experiments, but the hamlet of Alamogordo benefited even more from the demands of the war. Afterward, the Alamogordo Bombing Range (now White Sands Missile Range) commandeered an area larger than the state of Delaware. The largest range in the nation, it proved ideal for the postwar testing of captured German V-2 rockets. By 1958 the White Sands budget approached 160 million dollars, employing approximately 6,700 people. Steady technical demands from the Apollo program, the space shuttle program, and numerous energy contracts also helped transform nearby New Mexico State University into a major research institution. In 1976, Alamogordo dedicated an impressive Space Hall of Fame. It proudly called itself "Birthplace of Atomic Energy—Home of American Rocket Research."

The Very Large Array (VLA) radio telescope on the Plains of San Agustin, established in the mid-1970s, is the state's latest big science project. Here, amid grazing cattle and soaring falcons, astronomers maneuver six-story-high radio antennas to probe for the ultimate secrets of the universe. In 1989, the Cannon Air Force Base in Clovis was selected to house the nation's extensive F-111 fighter-bomber fleet. Such massive, federal expenditures have produced a genuine scientific subculture. On a per-capita basis, New Mexico has more scientific and technical workers than any other state. No area of New Mexico remains unaffected by this scientific world.

Since most of New Mexico science has involved defense measures or weapons production, the culture of big science has often carried with it a sense of moral ambiguity. On a personal level, the questions had relatively easy answers. People who were troubled about weapons work simply resigned. But on a community level, the questions proved more complex. During the late 1960s and early 1970s, anti-government protesters blocked the entrance gates to Albuquerque's Sandia Base and staged several marches in Los Alamos. Strangely, no group protested the open secret that the Manzano Mountains housed perhaps four hundred nuclear warheads.

The anti-war protesters pointed to the dark side of New Mexico's Culture of Science. To establish its various bases, the federal government had to confiscate the land of about one hundred families in the Socorro region and some two hundred others near Alamogordo. Most of these pioneers left peacefully but eighty-two-year-old John Prather, who owned land south of the Sacramento Mountains, refused to budge. In so doing, he became the symbol of crusty individual resistance to increasing federal encroachment. Fearing a scandal, the army allowed Prather to stay on his land until his death.

Other, less publicized incidents involved public safety. On May 22, 1957, an Air Force B-36 from Kirtland Base accidentally dropped a ten-megaton hydrogen bomb five miles south of Albuquerque, avoiding catastrophe only because the weapon was not fully armed. During the early 1970s, medical researchers concluded that Navajo uranium miners of the Four Corners area had been contracting lung cancer far above statistical norms; after almost two decades of agitation, President George Bush signed a compensation bill for them in the fall of 1990. The July 16, 1979, United Nuclear Corporation Church Rock Mill tailings pond rupture has the dubious distinction of being the worst radiation accident in all of American history. The 94 million gallons of radioactive liquid waste that washed into the Rio Puerco released far more radiation into the atmosphere than Pennsylvania's far better-known Three Mile Island disaster of the same year. It is another open secret that several canyons of Los Alamos contain numerous "hot spots" of buried waste that are decidedly "off limits."

Perhaps the ultimate symbol of the ambiguity of big science in New Mexico is the decade-long controversy over the Waste Isolation Pilot Project (WIPP), located twenty-six miles east of Carlsbad. In the early 1980s, scientists selected this ten-thousand-acre area of the state as the best possible site to store permanently the nation's low- and medium-level nuclear waste. According to theory, the region's underground salt formation had not only been stable for millennia, it would slowly "enfold" the nuclear waste (rather like plastic wrap) and thus keep it from ever entering the environment. Proponents of WIPP have also argued that it was ironically fitting that "the birthplace of the atomic age" should also hold its waste products. In spite of lengthy, vocal protests from merchants and environmental groups, the final WIPP legislation was passed by Congress in the fall of 1992.

With the close of the Cold War, plus increased concern for both energy issues and the environment, what does the future hold for New Mexico's culture of big science? The question defies easy answer. In the late 1980s the economy of Grants virtually collapsed; not even the most optimistic observer has predicted the resurgence of the uranium industry. Los Alamos, Kirtland, Sandia, and White Sands all suffered severe budget cutbacks in the 1980s and early 1990s. Since both Los Alamos and Sandia have always conducted a certain percentage of nondefense-research programs, many liberals have voiced hope that federal expenditures might shift to such areas as heat pumps, fusion power, algae farms, nuclear cleanup, nuclear safety, or cancer research. The ultimate symbol of this hope may be seen in the 57-million-dollar Clinton P. Anderson Meson facility that opened in Los Alamos in 1971. Whether this will occur or not hinges on two items: Congress's willingness to continue to fund expensive, nonmilitary-related research projects; and the transferable nature of the weapons scientists' skills. Whatever the future holds, however, the last half century of the Culture of Big Science has forever altered the New Mexico landscape. The state could never return to a prescience economy.

Third is the culture of tourism. In 1945, the Research Division of New Mexico's Committee for Economic Development published a study of future state economic growth. Concluding that expenditures for public-works projects could never provide a satisfactory economic base, the authors carefully explored the potential of agriculture, mining, oil and gas extraction, heavy manufacturing, light industries, and lumbering. Ironically, they hardly gave tourism a mention, even though prewar tourism had ranked as the state's leading source of cash income. Little has changed in the last fifty years. If one excludes the federal and state payrolls, in 1992 tourism still ranked as the main source of income and employment for the state. Recent estimates put the dollar amounts at 2.2 billion; over fifty-three thousand New Mexicans are somehow involved with tourism.

Originally part of the highway department, from the late 1930s forward the state Tourist Bureau did its best to acquaint the nation with the wonders of New Mexico. All sections of the state joined in this fifty-year crusade of self-promotion, some more effectively than others. But three sectors have parlayed their tourist appeal into a genuine international following. These were the Gallup Indian Ceremonial, the celebration of New Mexico skiing, and "the selling of Santa Fe."

In 1922, the border town of Gallup inaugurated its first Inter-tribal Indian Ceremonial "for an exhibit of Indian ceremonials, dances, sports, handicraft and agricultural and husbandry products." The ceremonial was established, said the articles of incorporation, for "mutual benefit and not for pecuniary profit or speculation." Aided by the post-World War II highway construction, Gallup became far more accessible to outsiders. The fall Ceremonial became the town's major attraction in the 1950s. Billing itself as "The Indian Capital of the World," Gallup entrepreneurs saw the Ceremonial as the fulfillment of a nineteenth-century Navajo trader's prophecy that "tourism is the pony that they'll [the Indians will] ride out on." Throughout the 1950s and 1960s, the Ceremonial put on traditional Native dances and arts displays. In addition, Gallup held conferences and speeches on Indian-related issues. By the early 1970s the festival drew in over thirty tribes, many from as far away as Mexico and Canada. The Indians utilized the Gallup gathering as a main stop on the "pow-wow circuit," and it became a standing Indian joke that the Ceremonial provided "an opportunity for Whites to see Indians and for Indians to see Indians, too." In 1970, just to pick a single year, the four days of celebration generated 1.5 million dollars in revenue for the Gallup area. Performances of the Buffalo Dance, Eagle Dance, Yeibichai dances, hoop dances, and others attracted a number of visitors, many coming from overseas.

In spite of the economic success, the Ceremonial faced a steady variety of complex problems. In 1954, Gallup police arrested almost one thousand of the eleven thousand people attending for public drunkenness. The Hopi tribe boycotted the Ceremonial for several years during the late 1950s, and Zuni pueblo governors periodically had to protest against Navajo plans to move the festival to Window Rock, Arizona. In 1969, militant members of the American Indian Movement (AIM) denounced the Ceremonial for exploiting Native Americans and tried to disrupt certain events. The next year, local newspapers were filled with talk about abandoning the Ceremonial entirely. Eventually, however, the town forged a compromise, part of which involved moving most activities to new grounds at the nearby Red Rock State Park. The local Pueblo and Navajo craftspeople strongly supported the Ceremonial, for it offered a convenient and profitable outlet for their workmanship. Tourist dollars produced by the celebration of Indian life proved essential to all of Gallup, regardless of ethnic affiliations.

In the late 1930s, northern New Mexico boasted several small ski areas in Las Vegas, Taos, and Santa Fe. But the "ski boom" that began in the late 1950s created a series of others, such as Red River (1959), Sierra Blanca, run by the Mescalero Apache tribe (1961), and Cloudcroft (1963), all of which relied heavily on Texas and Oklahoma visitors. Albuquerque's much debated aerial tram (1966) made her Sandia Peak more accessible to local skiers, too.

The central figure behind the state's postwar ski boom was Taos impresario Ernie Blake. A Swiss national, Blake (Bloch) served with Allied intelligence during World War II and arrived in the region in 1948 to manage the Santa Fe ski lift. Comparing northern New Mexico with the Alps, Blake set out on a two-year search to discover the perfect ski run. After careful surveying—including several low-level aerial flights over northern New Mexico and southern Colorado—Blake chose Twining, New Mexico, to create his Taos Ski Valley. Beginning in 1955, Blake steadily improved his area, adding chair lifts, French and Swiss chefs, boutiques, and the charm of a powerful and enigmatic personality. "Mr. Taos Ski Valley," as he was known, touted the region as "better than Switzerland," because of the dry, light snow, abundant sunshine, and lack of bitter cold. In large measure he succeeded. By the early 1970s, New Mexico's slopes had begun to attract skiers from all over the nation. Although the industry suffered setbacks in the 1980s, northern New Mexico still rivals Utah and Colorado for the best in intermountain American skiing.

The selling of Santa Fe, especially its world of crafts and fine arts, has become the most successful tourist tale of the postwar era. Although Taos and Santa Fe first achieved fame as art colonies around the turn of the century, the depression and the onset of the Second World War effectively brought those communities to an end. In 1945, for example, Santa Fe boasted only two art galleries, and well-known Taos artist Gustave Baumann regularly complained to Erna Fergusson, "Among the many problems that sit on my doorstep, the first one is to pay my way."

It took several decades for the art worlds to revive. In 1950, Albuquerque staged its first Annual All Albuquerque Artist's [sic] Exhibition. A Santa Fe art brochure of the same era felt it necessary to define such terms as "Impressionism," "Abstraction," and "Expressionism" for viewers. The brochure also warned that people should not view modern art "as a series of hoaxes perpetrated on an unsuspecting public by men who wish only to gain notoriety for themselves."

New Mexico's most celebrated native-born painter for the fifties and sixties was probably San Patricio's Peter Hurd. Working alongside his talented wife, Henriette Wyeth, Hurd captured the beauty and mystery of the twentieth-century Southwest in canvases such as *The Gate and Beyond* (1953). He also found himself in the national spotlight in 1967 when President Lyndon Johnson rejected Hurd's commissioned portrait as the "ugliest thing" he had ever seen. The Roswell Museum and Art Center contains the best collection of Hurd's work.

Less than a decade later, Lubbock native Forrest Fenn opened an art gallery across from the state capitol in Santa Fe, thus beginning the odyssey that would make him the Horatio Alger of the New Mexico art world. According to rumor, Fenn parlayed a twenty-five-thousand-dollar initial investment into

Peter Hurd interprets New Mexican ranch life in The Gate and Beyond. *(Courtesy Roswell Museum and Art Center.)*

a multimillion dollar operation. Fenn advised potential buyers that art was "just about foolproof" as an investment. He estimated that the best pieces would increase from 40 to 50 percent a year, and even offered refunds if they failed to appreciate. By 1980, Santa Fe contained about ninety art galleries, and Fenn Galleries claimed an annual volume of 6 million dollars. Simultaneously, Old Town in Albuquerque had twenty-four galleries; estimates put the Albuquerque art market at 12 million dollars a year. In 1990, Santa Fe had about 200 galleries. It also ranked third in the nation in art, trailing only New York City and Los Angeles. Significantly, it ranked first in the category of selling art to buyers outside of the region.

What were these tourists buying? The market fluctuated, of course, but initially the steady sales came from representational western themes, especially those depicting cowboys or Indians. These proved ever popular with the Oklahoma and Texas tourists. As an Albuquerque *Tribune* reporter noted in 1970, "the demand is so great for Old West art that many contemporary artists are busy turning out paintings and bronzes full of buffaloes, stage coaches, cattle drives and Indians. Yet few of these busy painters have ever seen a buffalo outside a zoo." When California tourists began to replace Oklahomans and Texans, Santa Fe galleries found they could market more abstract designs. Lithographs from the famed Tamarind Institute (which moved to Albuquerque in 1970) also became quite popular.

Some visitors purchased Hispanic crafts, such as the Chimayo weavings produced by the Ortega family, wood carvings, the micaceous pottery of Felipe Ortega, or pieces of furniture handmade by local craftspeople. The majority of tourists, however, preferred more "western" themes, especially those by Native American artists.

The culture of tourism provided American Indian artists with an increasing opportunity to market their work. Santa Clara Pueblo artist Pablita Velarde, and her daughter Helen Hardin, created both representational and abstract oil and earth paintings on Native themes. Choctaw Jerry Ingram's finely crafted horses and dancers also sold well. The sculptures of Chiricahua Apache Alan Houser filled many a tourist living room and local business, and virtually every New Mexican dreams of finding a María (Martínez) of San Ildefonso black-on-black pot at a New Jersey flea market for $2.50.

The success story of marketing Indian arts to the nation probably belongs to the colorful and controversial Navajo, R. C. Gorman of Taos. Born in Chinle on the reservation, Gorman moved to Taos to open his Navajo gallery and market his skillful, if sparse, drawings of Navajo life, usually of women. Flamboyant and sophisticated, Gorman sold himself as much as his artwork and soon became a local legend.

But has tourism in Santa Fe gone too far? In 1977, Santa Fe imposed a 3 percent lodgers' tax on local motels, hotels, and

San Ildefonso artist María Martínez fashions her world-famous black pottery by hand. (Courtesy Center for Southwest Research, General Library, University of New Mexico, neg. no. 000-099-1380.)

inns. This new tax flowed into a concerted campaign to advertise "The City Different" among the moneyed, East and West Coast "high rollers."

The campaign succeeded. In May 1981, *Esquire* magazine trumpeted Santa Fe as the place to be—"Great women, great weather, and plenty to do," blared the cover. The Denver *Post*, *People* and the "Today Show" picked up the chorus. Tourism soon became a year-round affair in Santa Fe. Shop owners who used to close for several months after Labor Day now began to hire extra help. Local newspapers touted tourism as a recession-proof industry.

One unforeseen dimension of increased tourism appeared

when many of these monied visitors decided to settle permanently in Santa Fe. The arrival of a number of film and media stars drew enormous attention. Writers Neil Simon, Sam Shepard, and Judy Blume moved to Santa Fe, as did entertainers such as Goldie Hawn, Robert Redford, Lily Tomlin, Roger Miller, Amy Irving, Jessica Lange, Don Meredith, and even the Duke and Duchess of Bedford. Population grew from forty thousand in 1970 to fifty thousand in 1980 to fifty-six thousand in 1990.

In 1988, *Megatrends* author John Naisbitt urged Santa Fe citizens to avoid industry for tourism and to continue to promote its "quality of life." But critics maintained that the rush of tourists was destroying the very thing that drew them there in the first place. Residents complained that Santa Fe had become "Aspenized," almost turned into an "Adobe Disneyland." The venerable Plaza stores gradually vacated the downtown area to relocate in various suburban malls. In their stead came high priced shops catering to the tourists, a "gallery ghetto" that ignored local citizens. Hispanics—40 percent of the town's population—virtually disappeared from the Plaza, to be replaced by publicity hungry "Plaza rats." "The area's cultural integrity," complained writer John Nichols, "is just getting blown away." Touted as "an elite oasis of grandeur, fame, big money and culture," Santa Fe became the second New Mexico city to achieve a worldwide reputation. It had become "America's Salzburg."

For the fourth point, I want to turn to a more traditional concept of culture: Education, *belles-lettres*, music, and religion. Historian Ronald Davis has argued that in contemporary Texas, there has been a continual battle between indigenous culture and imported "high" culture. Such a clash also occurred in New Mexico, but to a lesser extent. In New Mexico, the indigenous traditions all utilized the imported "high" culture for their own purposes.

In 1942, the U.S. Army asked the University of California at Berkeley to serve as a "cover" to order all equipment and pay all salaries for the scientists at Los Alamos. Some have wondered why the nearest school, the University of New Mexico in Albuquerque, was not tapped for this task. But in 1942, UNM had perhaps two thousand students and a faculty of under fifty. They could not possibly have disguised the vast quantities of matériel and personnel needed for Los Alamos.

Yet had Los Alamos been established in 1992, UNM most likely would have been selected for this role. By then it had grown to a school with twenty-six thousand students, several branch campuses, and international reputations in such fields as anthropology, Latin American Studies, and American Western History. The engineering and science departments all worked closely with the state's federal laboratories. New Mexico State University grew proportionately, and the regional colleges, such as Eastern New Mexico in Portales and Western New Mexico in Silver City, continued to serve local needs. New Mexico Highlands in Las Vegas emerged as "the Hispanic University" and continued to send many of its graduates into the political world. The University of New Mexico Press achieved a reputation as one of the best presses in the West. Although budgetary limitations hampered education on all levels, by 1992 the state had a sophisticated educational apparatus firmly in place.

The second area of "high culture" involved music. Although music played a major role in both traditional Indian and Spanish societies, prior to World War II few scholars had paid much attention to it. Pueblo Indian Manuel Archuleta began collecting Indian songs in the late 1940s, and even formed a company to produce Native American records. "The Tom Tom Family Dancers" did not sell well, however, as many non-Native buyers complained about the "monotony" of Indian music. In truth, Native performers often had to shorten their productions for their audiences. The market for Native music still lay in the future.

University of New Mexico music professor John Donald Robb almost singlehandedly revived interest in the state's Hispanic musical traditions. A graduate of Harvard Law School, Robb practiced his profession for twenty years before moving to New Mexico in 1941 to begin a second career in music. Traveling throughout the state, Robb set up his recorder at New Mexico weddings, sheepcamps, funerals, and campfires. He became fascinated with the blend of Hebrew, Moorish, and Gregorian chants that he found therein. In 1950, Robb drew on numerous Hispanic folksongs to compose an original opera, "The Life and Death of Little Jo." Termed Albuquerque's "Renaissance Man," Robb also founded and directed the first UNM symphony orchestra. In 1967, the opening of the Albuquerque Civic Light Opera Association added to the city's musical scene.

Several other cities, such as Roswell and Santa Fe, also began symphony orchestras, but the center of the state's post-war musical scene belonged to the "Miracle of the Desert": the Santa Fe Opera. The driving force behind the Opera was John Crosby, who in 1956-57 used 200,000 dollars of family monies to buy land north of the city and build a 470-seat wooden opera house on it.

In spite of dire predictions—"How can you sell an opera to people who have never heard one?"—Crosby persisted in his dream. To everyone's surprise, after a few years, the Opera began to play to full houses. In 1967, the old opera house burned—probably the result of arson—but Crosby turned even this disaster to an advantage. The cast finished the season in the local high school gym, and the next year Crosby oversaw the creation of an entirely new opera building that sat fourteen hundred people. In 1977, the mortgage was retired, right on schedule.

What began as a shoestring operation turned into the major musical institution for the entire West. Through an innovative apprentice program, Crosby brought in numerous young musicians, and a number of his "graduates" have gone on to major roles elsewhere. For years the Opera tried to balance traditional offerings—"Carmen," "Tosca," "Madame Butterfly"—with various world premiers. Since the 1960s, the Opera has proven to be one of Santa Fe's major attractions. Opening night invariably turns into a gala occasion. As Crosby reminded *New Yorker* writer Winthrop Sargeant, "Nations are not remembered for their bombers or their banking system. They are remembered for their art."

Like the world of music, New Mexican post-World War II *belles-lettres* soon moved from the provincial to the international. In the 1940s, the leading writer of the state was probably Erna Fergusson, widely acknowledged as the grande dame of New Mexico letters.The first person to reach national audiences with the "three-cultures" interpretation of the state's past, Fergusson argued in the 1950s that New Mexico's experience with multiculturalism should serve as a model for a United States that now found itself thrust into a world-leadership role. Drawing on her own girlhood experiences—where she heard English, Spanish, and German spoken in her family home—Fergusson argued that "the true New Mexico" had no room for prejudice. "New Mexico never had any real problems of intolerance or prejudice," she reminded an Albuquerque Kiwanis Club in 1959; "everybody got along perfectly well with everybody else." Fergusson's contemporary, Santa Fe author Dorothy L. Pillsbury, argued along equally rosy lines. She emphasized the theme of cultural harmony in numerous well-written essays. In the works of Fergusson and Pillsbury, the New Mexico story remained shrouded in romance. This would change considerably over time.

The immediate postwar literary world also included a number of historians. One of the most prolific, C. L. Sonnichsen, began his career as a professor of literature at the University of Texas at El Paso (UTEP; then Texas Western) in 1931. Within two decades, Sonnichsen had become the chief historical writer of southern New Mexican life. Calling himself a "grassroots historian," Sonnichsen sought out both old newspapers and old-timers to piece together his tales of *Alias Billy the Kid* (1955), *Mescalero Apaches* (1958), and *Tularosa: Last of the Frontier West* (1960). But Sonnichsen was not alone. The Reverend Francis Stanley Crocchiola (writing as F. Stanley); Jack Rittenhouse, who established his own Stagecoach Press; and longtime state historian Myra Ellen Jenkins also added considerably to local history during the first decades after the war. So, too, did Marc Simmons, prolific author of over twenty books on New Mexican themes, including a history of Albuquerque and the bicentennial volume on the state.

The most popular historian of New Mexico, however, was the multitalented Fray Angelico Chavez. A Franciscan priest who served several New Mexico parishes, Chavez wrote two major works, *Missions of New Mexico, 1776* (with Eleanor B. Adams), and *Origins of New Mexico Families in the Spanish Colonial Period* (1973). Chavez probably reached the widest audience with his evocative *My Penitente Land* (1974), which compared New Mexico with central Spain in perceptive and graceful prose.

During the 1970s and 1980s, Santa Fe writer Stan Steiner

brought the West in general, and New Mexico in particular, to the attention of the nation with thirteen books, including *The New Indians* (1975), *La Raza* (1970), *The Vanishing White Man* (1976), and *The Ranchers* (1980). Until his death, Steiner was hailed as the major interpreter of the "New West."

The sophistication of literature grew in step with the sophistication of historical writing. In 1960, when bookman Lawrence Clark Powell was asked to compile a "best books on New Mexico" list, he faced an embarrassment of riches. Yet the state literary renaissance had hardly begun. In 1966, playwright Mark Medoff moved to Las Cruces to teach at New Mexico State. His *Children of a Lesser God* won numerous awards and became a popular film. Albuquerque playwright James (Grubb) Graebner achieved off-Broadway success with several plays, including *The Great White Atomic Sweepstakes*.

Prior to 1960, most of the major books dealing with Native American themes, such as Oliver La Farge's *Laughing Boy* (1929), had been written by non-Indians. During the sixties, however, the state's Native voice began to be heard in several genres. Acoma poet Simon Ortiz collected his poems in *From Sand Creek* (1981), while N. Scott Momaday, who grew up at Jemez Pueblo, won a Pulitzer Prize for *House Made of Dawn* (1968). Laguna writer Leslie Marmon Silko achieved international fame with her novel *Ceremony* (1977). In general, these were not happy voices.

During the same period, a number of Spanish-American writers consciously began to inaugurate a revived Hispanic literature. No one represented this theme better than UNM English professor Rudolfo Anaya. Author of several studies of New Mexico Hispanic life, Anaya's *Bless Me, Ultima* (1974) told of a young man's coming of age in a small Hispanic village. As a former dean of the College of Arts and Sciences at the University recently observed, "Many UNM professors have

Choctaw artist Jerry Ingram illustrates Native American religious practices in
Sacred Manner. (Courtesy of the artist.)

written books, but Rudolfo Anaya is one of the few about whom
books have been written." Western literary critics agree that
Gretel Ehrlich has captured the spirit of Wyoming in The Solace
of Open Spaces (1985); they acknowledge that Ivan Doig has
caught the vastness of Montana in This House of Sky (1972);
they are in similar agreement that Rudolfo Anaya has pinned
down the elusive spirit of New Mexico in Bless Me, Ultima. In
the 1990s there is no question that New Mexico writers have
come of age.

The multiplicity of views that one finds in the state's
literature was even more prevalent in the story of religion in
New Mexico. At the end of the war, New Mexico's religious
scene was dominated by a predominantly Hispanic Catholic
congregation served by Irish or French priests; a variety of
Native faiths, both mingled with, and separate from, this

Catholicism; a deep-rooted German Jewish community; and most of the mainline Protestant groups, led by the Presbyterians. Fifty years later, New Mexico had become a "spiritual land" that attracted both conventional and unconventional groups in large numbers. The 1990s religious scene lay in such flux that few dared predict its outcome.

Even in the 1950s, New Mexico boasted a number of monasteries and religious conference centers. In 1955, Trappist monks established a retreat in the Pecos Mountains, but it did not thrive until 1969 when a band of Benedictine monks purchased the property and changed it drastically. The Pecos Benedictine Abbey became the only coed Catholic monastery in the states, combining a Jungian psychology with an emphasis on Catholic charismatic worship. The Benedictines also established a more traditional monastery of Christ in the Desert, near Abiquiu, with a dramatic chapel designed by architect George Nakashima. In nearby Jemez Springs, the church has operated (since 1947) the Monastery of Via Coeli, devoted to aiding priests with personal and spiritual problems.

The Protestants have also established two impressive conference centers in northern New Mexico: the Presbyterian Ghost Ranch and the Southern Baptist Glorieta Assembly. The former, near Abiquiu, was donated to the church by rancher Arthur N. Park, while the latter was constructed in the Pecos Mountains in the early 1950s under the leadership of Harry Stagg. By the 1990s, the Southern Baptists dominated the state's Protestant community. They claimed more members than all the rest of the Protestants put together. In the southern section of the state, the West Texas Bloys Camp Meeting continued to influence regional religious life.

Since the late 1960s, however, the northern part of New Mexico has attracted a number of very distinct religious groups. In the early 1970s, a Sikh community began in the Española

Valley. The ashram of about two hundred people became the group's international headquarters in 1976. The community members' white turbans; their emphasis on physical and spiritual health; and their role in local security businesses have given them a high regional profile. A mosque, Dar-al-Islam, was also established near Abiquiu, lasting from the early to the late 1980s. A small but thriving Zen center exists in Santa Fe. The New Age movement, probably best understood as an eclectic questing for spirituality, has also found a permanent home in "The City Different." At last count, Santa Fe listed ninety-five acupuncturists, making it a haven for holistic healing practitioners from a wide variety of faith positions.

The preeminent postwar state religious figures, however, have probably been two Catholic spokesmen, Brother Mathias Barrett and Archbishop Robert F. Sanchez. An Irish immigrant, Brother Mathias established his first house of the Little Brothers of the Good Shepherd in 1951 in Albuquerque. Dedicated to serving the needs of the desperately poor, Brother Mathias's order is now found worldwide.

Born in Socorro, the Reverend Robert F. Sanchez became New Mexico's tenth archbishop in 1974, the first native-born Hispanic to hold this post. On the national level, Sanchez was well respected for his advocacy of justice for minorities, the impoverished, and, especially, for the people of Latin America. On the local level, "the people's bishop," as his parishioners called him, was genuinely beloved. Both Protestants and Catholics respected his administrative skills, compassion, and wit. On one occasion Sanchez remarked that the Catholic Church in New Mexico had such deep roots "we could have been saying Mass for the safety of the Pilgrims."

Given this affection, New Mexicans were stunned in early 1993 when accusations began to surface that the archbishop had been sexually involved with perhaps five different women during the 1970s and early 1980s, a story prominently featured on CBS-TV's "60 Minutes" program. February and March thus provided some of the most wrenching weeks in the lengthy history of the New Mexico church. When Sanchez resigned his post on March 20, the New Mexico State House and Senate recessed for thirty minutes out of respect. The next Sunday several Protestant ministers prayed for the state's Catholic populace. Just before Easter, the Pope appointed Lubbock, Texas, Bishop Michael J. Sheehan to be temporary administrator of the Santa Fe Archdiocese, and Sheehan also urged that Robert Sanchez's failings not overshadow "the untold amount of good" that he had accomplished during his nineteen years of leadership. Experts predicted, however, that repercussions from this incident would be felt for years.

In spite of this, by the early 1990s New Mexico had become a "spiritual magnet." The state seemed to draw in seekers from every religious group imaginable. As a Sikh leader recently observed, "God lives everywhere, but his mailing address is New Mexico."

In the Spring of 1991, two young New Mexicans stopped for gasoline in Yakima, Washington. When the station attendant noticed their license, she asked, "What's the difference between Mexico and New Mexico?" Virtually every long-term resident has had a similar experience. Since 1969, *New Mexico Magazine* has run a regular column detailing these misunderstandings. In 1986, Richard Sandoval collected these misconceptions in a popular booklet, *One of Our Fifty Is Missing.*

Popular culture, the last of the post-World War II "cultures" to be discussed, has tried to ameliorate this situation. But until recently, even New Mexico's popular culture has grappled with problems of recognition.

From 1950 to the present day, the state's most famous citizen has been neither man nor woman. Instead, the most famous New Mexican has been a bear, a small cub who lost his mother in the 1950 El Capitan Mountain forest fire in the Lincoln National Forest. The bear in question, of course, was Smokey, who has reminded the nation for over forty years that "only you can prevent forest fires." Surveys showed that 95 percent of American children could correctly identify Smokey's image. No New Mexican, before or since, has done as well.

Ironically, however, while everyone recognized Smokey, few connected the real, live bear who lived out his life rather grumpily in a cage at the Washington National Zoo with the smiling cartoon figure in Levis and Ranger hat. Even New Mexico's most famous citizen, alas, is seldom linked with the land of his birth.

The same problem of recognition lay behind the decision by Hot Springs, New Mexico, to alter its name. In early 1950, NBC impresario Ralph Edwards promised to stage his tenth-anniversary broadcast from any town that changed its name to "Truth or Consequences," the title of his radio show. The small community of Hot Springs, located on the edge of Elephant Butte Lake, elected to do so. Edwards not only kept his promise, he returned to T. or C. for over two decades to oversee an annual fiesta, well after his show had gone to media heaven. Three times various town conservatives have tried to restore the original name, but three times they failed. Ironically, although Truth or Consequences boasts New Mexico's most unusual name, few people under thirty connect it with anything other than local eccentricity.

If the state's most famous citizen is a bear and the most uniquely labeled city named for a radio show, New Mexico's most famous vegetable is, botanically, a fruit: the ubiquitous chile. Like the others, the chile's quest for recognition is also very much a postwar phenomenon.

The 1945 state economic forecast neglected to mention

chile as an important agricultural crop. As late as 1955, the major chile under production, New Mexico No. 9, proved far too *picante* for sale anywhere outside the state. Shortly afterward, Roy Nakayama, botanist at New Mexico State, began working with local ranchers, such as Jim Lytle of Hatch, to improve the taste and quality. Crossbreeding from both native as well as rare Peruvian chiles, Nakayama masterminded the commercial production of NuMex Big Jim in the fall of 1974. Bred to produce pods about a foot long, Big Jims also matured simultaneously, making them ideal for machine picking. On a hotness scale, with mild New Mexico 6 as "1" and tabasco as "9," NuMex Big Jim was ranked a "3," almost ideal for the average palate. By the 1980s, New Mexico grew more acres of chile than all other states combined, and the annual Hatch Chile Festival had achieved a modest national reputation. Thanks to the genius of Roy Nakayama and his colleague at NMSU, Paul Bosland, New Mexico now exports millions of pounds of chile per year, all across the land. As Mexican food is currently the second fastest growing of all ethnic cuisines (Italian is first), can the ultimate fame of New Mexican chile be far behind?

Film and video probably lie at the heart of any discussion of popular culture. Interestingly, New Mexico has had a long-standing connection with the film industry. During the early years of the century, Las Vegas hosted a number of western epics. But producers soon moved on to the sunny shores of Hollywood, and for years the state wallowed in a cinema backwater.

The first postwar film to treat New Mexico in any detail was probably *Them*, a 1954 classic about ants that had been transformed into giant mutants by walking across Ground Zero at Trinity Site. Although many of the scenes from this gem were shot in Arizona—where saguaro cacti served as the symbol of "desert"—the story was largely a New Mexican one. The first of the "mutant movies," the giant ants of *Them* brought New Mexico to the attention of the nation, although probably not in the way that the chamber of commerce would have preferred.

In 1968, Governor David Cargo decided to ameliorate this situation. That year, he established the first state film commission in the nation. Soon, New Mexican bureaucrats were badgering Hollywood producers to shoot their next films in the state. To further encourage the studios, the government built a state-owned sound stage, which it leased out at bargain-basement prices. Nearby communities, such as Cerrillos, welcomed filmmakers, and state cooperation even extended to loaning state police for traffic control and letting Albuquerque school children out of class for needed crowd scenes. Whenever local stories were filmed, such as *Red Sky at Morning* and *House Made of Dawn*, the New Mexico press gave the films wide coverage. From 1968 to 1988, Hollywood shot over 150 films on location in New Mexico. Hollywood spending in the state increased steadily, from eight million in 1983-84 to over thirty million four years later. New Mexico's film commission also served as a model for other states.

Although certain films such as *Easy Rider* contained some New Mexican scenes, the most celebrated state film was *The Milagro Beanfield War* (1986). Based on Taos writer John Nichols's novel of 1972, *Milagro* starred Sonia Braga, Freddie Fender, and Ruben Blades; Robert Redford both produced and directed it. After the citizens of Cordova turned Redford down, he moved to Truchas for the brunt of the filming, creating an artificial beanfield with plastic plants as his main backdrop. Turning a 629-page book into a 123-minute movie proved challenging. While local reviewers termed *Milagro* "five star" and "the best movie ever made in the state," nationwide reaction was less enthusiastic. *Milagro* showed marvelous New Mexico scenery, but it never turned the state into the hoped-for "Hollywood on the Rio Grande."

From 1945 to the present, New Mexican sports figures have also brought the state into the national eye. In auto racing, the famous Unsers, Al and Bobby, became the only brothers ever to win the Indianapolis 500. In the 1980s, their sons followed them into the same profession. Roswell's Nancy Lopez dominated womens' professional golf during the early 1980s, and endeared herself to the state by her charm of personality. In track, the exploits of world-class runners like Adolph Plummer; John Baker, of whom the book *A Shining Season* (1978) was written; and Ibrahim Hussein (who won the Boston Marathon twice) commanded a wide following. The most widespread national publicity, however, came not from individual but team sports, chiefly college basketball.

From the early 1960s forward, both the UNM Lobos and the NMSU Aggies fielded increasingly competitive basketball teams. New stadiums helped: the UNM Arena (The Pit) held 15,000 when it was completed in 1967; the Pan American Center, finished the next year, seated 13,272. Aided by lucrative television revenue, college basketball soon became the state's most popular sport, with the equivalent of one-third of the population each year attending a game. In 1978, *New Mexico Magazine* proudly proclaimed the state as "the basketball capital of the world." Even the 1979-80 scandals of UNM'S "Lobogate," with falsified transcripts and allegations of gambling, failed to dampen the public's enthusiasm. The holding of the NCAA Basketball finals in Albuquerque in 1983 symbolized the importance of the sport on both the local and national level.

A number of local mass market writers have also steadily moved New Mexico into the public eye. In 1956, Albuquerque writer Ray Hogan published his first western novel, and over the next thirty-five years turned out over 143 others, many set in the state. His contemporary, Portales writer Jack Williamson, achieved an international reputation in the field of science fiction. Writer Jack Schaefer moved to New Mexico in 1954 to produce a number of works, although none matched his 1949 masterpiece, *Shane*. In 1968, Edward Abbey reached his widest audience with *Desert Solitaire*, a story of his two seasons as a ranger in Utah's Arches National Park. Abbey's *The Monkey Wrench Gang* (1975) is usually credited with inaugurating the concept of "eco-terrorism," a practice he began—by chopping down billboards on Route 66—when he was a graduate student at UNM in the late 1950s. Albuquerque writer Lois Duncan has made New Mexico the locus of several of her juvenile fiction works, including *They Never Came Home* (1969) and *Ransom* (1984); Norman Zollinger's *Riders to Cibola* (1979) treats southern New Mexico; Judith Van Giesen is off to a good start with her Albuquerque female detective, Niel Hammel, in *Raptor* (1990) and *The Other Side of Death* (1991).

No discussion of modern New Mexican culture would be complete without mention of artist Georgia O'Keeffe and author Tony Hillerman. Both have transcended the boundaries between "high" and "popular culture." And both are forever linked with the New Mexican landscape.

Born in Wisconsin, O'Keeffe trained as a commercial artist and taught art both in South Carolina and Texas. In 1916, she met photographer Alfred Stieglitz, with whom her name would forever be associated. They began living together in 1918 and married in 1924. O'Keeffe fell in love with New Mexico on her first visit in 1917; she moved to Abiquiu permanently in 1949. Well before her death in Santa Fe in 1986, critics had dubbed her America's most original artist; the nation's greatest woman painter; perhaps "the greatest woman painter in the world."

Ironically, until about 1975 O'Keeffe was probably more famous nationally than in her adopted state. Dressed in a long black gown, she would often be recognized shopping in Santa Fe, but her Hispanic neighbors in Abiquiu generally marked her out as an eccentric, best left alone. (In gratitude for this, she built a fifty-thousand-dollar gymnasium for the town.) The UNM Fine Arts Museum did not stage O'Keeffe's first in-state exhibit until 1966; Santa Fe did not follow with her second show until 1975. Not until the Santa Fe Chamber Music Festival began to use O'Keeffe reprints as popular posters in the early 1970s did New Mexicans come to appreciate her talents. As late as 1975, a reporter observed that while O'Keeffe's fame was international, she was probably one of New Mexico's least-known residents.

If local residents ignored Georgia O'Keeffe, the national art critics did not. Except for her larger-than-life images of flowers—most of which were done before she moved to New Mexico—critics invariably linked her with the southwestern landscape. They delighted in her description of the Sangre de Cristo Mountains as "miles of grey elephants" or her assessment of New Mexico's light as "the faraway nearby." Her bleached cow skulls and her numerous renditions of Pedernal Mountain ("It's *my* mountain") have confirmed that impression. *Her Black Cross, New Mexico* (1929), one of the first canvases she painted in the state, completed the identification. As a reporter noted in 1968, Georgia O'Keeffe had become the virtual symbol of the American Southwest.

An Oklahoma native, Tony Hillerman moved to Santa Fe as a United Press bureau manager and later became editor of the *New Mexican*. After moving to Albuquerque, where he served as assistant to two UNM presidents and as head of the Journalism Department, Hillerman decided to try his hand at mystery writing. His first mystery, *The Blessing Way* (1970), astounded readers with its graceful language, haunting descriptions of the Navajo reservation, and the detective skill of his hero, Lt. Joe Leaphorn of the Navajo Tribal Police. As one perceptive reviewer noted, the author "has opened a Pandora's box for himself, for no one who reads this book is going to permit him to forget that we want more."

Hillerman proved as prolific as he was skilled. His *Dance Hall of the Dead* (1973) won the coveted Edgar Award from the Mystery Writers Association and the last four of his ten books, *Coyote Waits* (1990), *Talking God* (1989), *A Thief of Time* (1988), and *Skinwalkers* (1986), have all made the *New York Times* best-seller list. He has also been translated into numerous languages. Literary critics agree that Tony Hillerman has been writing the best mystery novels in the nation for over a decade. Robert Redford has taken film options on all his books, with the first one (*The Dark Wind*) available on video cassette. Hillerman's Navajo detectives Joe Leaphorn and Jim Chee have introduced millions of readers to the Southwest in general and the Navajo reservation in particular.

From Boston and New York to Chinle and Window Rock, Hillerman fans devour his books with glee. Once when the author asked a Navajo youth if he'd read any of his works, the boy replied, "Mr. Hillerman, I've got to either read your books or drop out of school." But even more telling is a comment from a Pima, Arizona, reservation librarian. She and Hillerman were speaking of the works of the nation's major Native writers when the woman said, "We read their books and say, this is beautiful and this is us, but they're so sad. They're so full of sorrow and loss and despair. But then we read your books and we say, 'This is us too and we win.'" Popular culture can hardly do more.

The rise of the post-World War II "cultures" of landscape, science, tourism, high culture, and popular culture have transformed modern New Mexico. In many and subtle ways, they have intersected with the famed "Heroic Triad" of the Native American, Hispanic, and Anglo-Pioneer worlds. Few would disagree that the charm and uniqueness of New Mexico may be traced to the interaction of its various cultures. Now the question is: which cultures?

BIBLIOGRAPHY

The term *culture* is a slippery one, and most historians have given it wide berth. Sitting down with the last half-century of *New Mexico Magazine* would probably provide the best introduction to the shifting "cultures of modern New Mexico." For those with time restraints, however, the following books also discuss the theme.

Most state histories, such as Calvin and Susan Roberts, *New Mexico* (Albuquerque: University of New Mexico Press, 1988), and Frank D. Reeve and Alice Ann Cleaveland, *New Mexico: Land of Many Cultures* (Boulder: Pruett Publishing Company, 1969), have appropriate sections. The broad concept of culture is explored in more depth in Marta Weigle and Peter White, eds., *The Lore of New Mexico* (Albuquerque: University of New Mexico Press, 1988), and, piecemeal, in *New Mexico: A New Guide to the Colorful State* (Albuquerque: University of New Mexico Press, 1989).

THE ARTS   Ever since the early twentieth century, New Mexico has had a close connection with the art world. A. M. Gibson, *The Santa Fe and Taos Colonies: Age of the Muses, 1900–1942* (Norman: University of Oklahoma Press, 1983), details the origins of this movement, but there is no comparable survey for the post–World War II era. Consequently, one must go largely to biographies of individual artists. Roswell native Paul Horgan discusses San Patricio's Peter Hurd in *Peter Hurd: A Portrait Sketch from Life* (Austin: University of Texas Press, 1965), while the artist's early work is available in Peter Hurd, *Portfolio of Landscapes and Portraits* (Albuquerque: University of New Mexico Press, 1950). The Roswell

Museum and Art Center contains the best collection of Hurd's work, as well as that of this talented wife, Henriette Wyeth.

The most famous contemporary Indian women artists are treated in Sally Hyer, "Pablita Velarde," in Margaret Connell Szasz, ed., *The Cultural Broker: Link Between Indian and White Worlds* (Norman: University of Oklahoma Press, forthcoming), and Alice Lee Marriott, *María: The Potter of San Ildefonso* (Norman: University of Oklahoma Press, 1968).

The state's most celebrated painter, Georgia O'Keeffe, has been the subject of three recent biographies: Laurie Lisle, *Portrait of an Artist: A Biography of Georgia O'Keeffe* (Albuquerque: University of New Mexico Press, 1986); Roxana Robinson, *Georgia O'Keeffe: A Life* (New York: Harper and Row, 1989); and Benita Eisler, *O'Keeffe and Stieglitz: An American Romance* (New York: Doubleday, 1991). New Mexico's Tamarind Institute and its role in the revival of lithography may be found in Garo Antreasian and Clinton Adams, *The Tamarind Book of Lithography: Art and Techniques* (New York: Harry N. Abrams, 1971).

In addition to painting, the world of art photography has an important history in New Mexico. One should begin with Van Deren Coke's *Photography in New Mexico: From the Daguerreotype to the Present* (Albuquerque: University of New Mexico Press, 1979). For images by the best New Mexico photographers, see Laura Gilpin, *The Pueblos: A Camera Chronicle* (New York: Hastings House, 1941); Gilpin, *The Enduring Navajo* (Austin: University of Texas Press, 1965); and Ernest Knee, *Santa Fe, New Mexico* (New York: Hastings House, 1942).

The two foremost nature photographers of the twentieth century, Eliot Porter and Ansel Adams, both have strong New Mexico links. For Porter, see *Eliot Porter's Southwest* (New York: Holt, Rinehart and Winston, 1985); and for Adams, *Ansel Adams: Images, 1923– 1974*, foreword by Wallace Stegner (Boston: New York Graphic Society, 1974), and James Alinder, *Ansel Adams: Classic Images* (Boston: Little, Brown, 1986).

The University of New Mexico Press has achieved an international reputation in the field of photography books. The variety of the photographic wing of UNM Fine Arts Department may be seen in two recent studies: *Silver Lining: Photographs by Anne Noggle* (Albuquerque: University of New Mexico Press, 1983), and Patrick Nagatani's *Nuclear Enchantment* (Albuquerque: University of New Mexico Press, 1991). As one contemporary eastern photographer observed, New Mexico has become "almost synonymous with photography."

ARCHITECTURE   Four UNM Press books detail the story of contemporary state architecture. Bainbridge Bunting, *Of Earth and Timbers Made: New Mexico Architecture* (1974), provides a good introduction to the subject. Bunting also wrote a study of the state's most influential architect in *John Gaw Meem: Southwestern Architect* (Albuquerque: University of New Mexico Press, 1983); Carl D. Sheppard has penned *Creator of the Santa Fe Style: Isaac Hamilton Rapp, Architect* (Albuquerque: University of New Mexico Press, 1988). The most controversial state architect is the subject of a study by Christopher Mead, *Houses by Bart Prince: An American Architecture for the Continuous Present* (Albuquerque: University of New Mexico Press, 1991).

SCIENCE   Big Science has shaped modern New Mexico in a myriad of ways. One should begin with David M. Hsi et al., eds., *From Sundaggers to Space Exploration—Significant Contributions to Science and Technology in New Mexico*, special issue of the *New Mexico Journal of Science* 26 (February 1986). Ever since 1942, the state has been linked with the Atomic Age, a theme discussed in several books: James W. Kunetka, *City of Fire: Los Alamos and the Atomic Age* (Albuquerque: University of New Mexico Press, 1979); Ferenc Morton Szasz, *The Day the Sun Rose Twice: The Story of the Trinity Site Nuclear Explosion, July 16, 1945* (Albuquerque: University of New Mexico Press, 1984); Raye C. Ringholz, *Uranium Frenzy: Boom and Bust on the Colorado Plateau* (New York: Norton, 1989); and Necah Stewart Furman, *Sandia National Laboratories: The Post War Decade* (Albuquerque: University of New Mexico Press, 1990). C. L. Sonnichsen analyzes the impact of the White Sands Missile

Range on the Tularosa Basin in his *Pilgrim in the Sun* (El Paso: The University of Texas at El Paso, 1988).

LITERATURE   If *culture* is understood to include serious historical writing and literature, New Mexico writers have achieved real maturity since 1942. Historian Erna Fergusson paved the way with her *New Mexico: A Pageant of Three Peoples* (New York: Knopf, 1951), a theme picked up by Paul Horgan in *The Heroic Triad: Essays in the Social Energies of Three Southwestern Cultures* (New York: Holt, Rinehart and Winston, 1970). Prolific author Marc Simmons has penned a brief state survey in *New Mexico* (New York: Norton, 1977).

The contemporary Native American voice may be found in Simon Ortiz, *From Sand Creek* (New York: Thunder Mouth Press, 1981); N. Scott Momaday, *House Made of Dawn* (New York: Harper and Row, 1968); and Leslie Marmon Silko, *Ceremony* (New York: Viking, 1977). The foremost Hispanic writer of the present day is Rudolfo Anaya, whose *Bless Me, Ultima* (Berkeley: Tonatiuh International, 1972) is now acknowledged as a New Mexico classic.

Other writers who have captured the spirit of the region include Angelico Chavez, *My Penitente Land: Reflections on Spanish New Mexico* (Albuquerque: University of New Mexico Press, 1974), and UNM graduate Edward Abbey, whose chronicle of his two years as a ranger at Arches National Park in Utah, *Desert Solitaire: A Season in the Wilderness* (New York: McGraw Hill, 1968), has probably reached the widest audience.

RELIGION AND MUSIC   In the field of modern religious history, see Richard W. Etulain, ed., *Religion in the Twentieth-Century American West: A Bibliography* (Albuquerque: University of New Mexico, Center for the American West, 1991). The story of the state's largest Protestant group may be found in David H. Stratton, *The First Century of Baptists in New Mexico* (Albuquerque: Woman's Missionary Union of New Mexico, 1954), which carries the tale to 1950; the most prominent contemporary Baptist is also the subject of a biography by Bonnie Ball O'Brien, *Harry P. Stagg: Christian Statesman* (Nashville: Broadman, 1976). Neither the Presbyterians, Methodists, nor Roman Catholics have written modern religious state histories, but Carol Lovato has detailed the life of New Mexico's most prominent post-World War II religious figure in *Brother Mathias: Founder of the Little Brothers of the Good Shepherd* (Huntington, Md.: Our Sunday Visitor, 1987). Henry Tobias, *A History of the Jews in New Mexico* (Albuquerque: University of New Mexico Press, 1990), carries the story up to the present day.

There is no overview of music in New Mexico. Ned Sublette, however, has compiled *A Discography of Hispanic Music in the Fine Arts Library of the University of New Mexico* (Westport, Conn.: Greenwood Press, 1973). Since the late 1950s, the Santa Fe Opera has achieved worldwide fame. On this, see Ronald L. Davis, *A History of Opera in the American West* (Englewood Cliffs, N.J.: Prentice-Hall, 1965), and, especially, Eleanor Scott, *The First Twenty Years of the Santa Fe Opera* (Santa Fe: Sunstone Press, 1976).

POPULAR CULTURE   "Popular culture" is, perhaps, the most elusive aspect of any discussion of contemporary cultural traditions. Melinda M. Snodgrass has edited *A Very Large Array: New Mexico Science Fiction and Fantasy* (Albuquerque: University of New Mexico Press, 1987); and Richard C. Sandoval has compiled a delightful collection of outside misunderstandings of the state in *One of Our Fifty Is Missing* (Santa Fe: *New Mexico Magazine*, 1986).

Albuquerque bookseller Norman Zollinger has garnered a following for his New Mexican western novels, especially *Riders to Cibola* (Santa Fe: Museum of New Mexico Press, 1979). Judith Van Giesen has created an intriguing Albuquerque female detective, Niel Hammel, in *Raptor* (1990) and *The Other Side of Death* (New York: Harper Collins, 1991).

Of course, popular mystery writer Tony Hillerman stands in a class by himself. The last four of his ten books, *Coyote Waits* (1990), *Talking God* (1989), *A Thief of Time* (1988), and *Skinwalkers* (1986), have all made the *New York Times* best-seller list. Through his works, millions of readers have become acquainted with the various cultural traditions of the American Southwest.

NOTES ON THE EDITOR
AND CONTRIBUTORS

Richard W. Etulain is Professor of History and Director of the Center for the American West at the University of New Mexico. Specializing in cultural history and historiography, he has authored or edited several books on the West. Among his recent volumes are *The American West: A Twentieth-Century History* (with Michael P. Malone, 1989), *The Twentieth-Century West: Historical Interpretations* (with Gerald D. Nash, 1989), *Conversations with Wallace Stegner* (rev. ed., 1990), and *Writing Western History* (1991). He edits or coedits four series and is working on a cultural history of the modern American West.

F. Chris Garcia is Professor of Political Science at the University of New Mexico, where he teaches courses in American politics, public opinion and electoral behavior, and Hispanics in U.S. politics. His works include coediting three editions of *New Mexico Government* (1976, 1981, and 1992); coauthoring *State and Local Government in New Mexico* (1979), with Paul Hain and Hal Rhodes; *The Chicano Political Experience*, with Rodolfo de la Garza (1974); and *Latinos and the Political System* (1988). He is currently analyzing and reporting the data from a major national attitudinal research project, the Latino National Political Survey.

Gerald D. Nash is Distinguished Professor of History at the University of New Mexico, where he teaches courses in U. S. and western twentieth-century history. Among his publications in these fields are *The American West in the Twentieth Century* (1973), *The American West Transformed: The Impact of World War II* (1985), *World War II and the West: Reshaping the Economy* (1990), and *Creating the West: Historical Interpretations, 1890-1990* (1991). He is currently completing a book on the military-industrial complex in the American West.

Rosalie Otero is Acting Director of the General Honors Program at the University of New Mexico. In addition to her administrative duties, Dr. Otero also teaches seminars in Honors. Interested in multicultural and gender issues, she has presented papers on these topics at national conferences and for local organizations. She has written several short stories, including "Las Dos Hermanas," in *The Third Woman*, ed. Dexter Fisher (Houghton Mifflin, 1980); and "The Closet," in *Las Mujeres Hablan*, ed. Tey Diana Rebolledo, Erlinda Gonzales-Berry, and Teresa Márquez (El Norte Publications, 1988). She is currently completing a reference guide, *American Drama, 1942–1992* (G. K. Hall-Macmillan). Dr. Otero is a native New Mexican.

Virginia Scharff is Assistant Professor of History at the University of New Mexico, where she teaches courses in U.S. social history and women's history. Her publications include *Taking the Wheel: Women and the Coming of the Motor Age* (1991); and *Present Tense: The United States since 1945* (1992), with Michael Schaller and Robert Schulzinger. She also writes about women in the western United States. She is currently working on a book about the counterculture of the 1960s and 1970s.

Ferenc M. Szasz, Professor of History at the University of New Mexico, specializes in social and cultural history. He has published several books and numerous essays on a variety of topics. Among his publications in religious history are *The Divided Mind of Protestant America* (1982) and *The Protestant Clergy in the Great Plains and*

Mountain West (1988). He has also written about the Trinity site in *The Day the Sun Rose Twice* (1984) and has recently authored *British Scientists and The Manhattan Project: The Los Alamos Years* (1992). He is presently at work on other books on religion and science in the West.

Michael Welsh is Assistant Professor of History at the University of North Colorado, where he teaches courses in the environment and cultures of the West and Southwest. His publications include *The U.S. Army Corps of Engineers: Albuquerque District, 1935–1985* (1987); and the forthcoming *Servants of the Golden Dream: The South Pacific Division, U.S. Army Corps of Engineers, 1840–1990.* He is currently completing a study of the University of New Mexico from 1889 to 1940.

INDEX

Note: Boldface numerals indicate an extended treatment of the subject.